THE
IN-BETWEEN
YEARS

by

Dorothea Desforges

Published by Buttercup Press
South Cave, East Yorkshire, HU15 2JG

First published in Great Britain 2001

ISBN0-9539190-3-X

Gem Desk Top Publishing
Welton, East Yorkshire, HU15 1NP

INTRODUCTION

This book is witness to five extraordinary years as an evacuee in the Canadian prairies.

Even though the life was harsh and my relatives battled endlessly with hail, drought, crop failure, extreme weather and poverty, the over-riding emotion was happiness, not the beatings and sorrow that is well documented in many other evacuee stories.

Whilst it is true that memory tends to select only the very interesting or disreputable, it can easily be persuaded, with a few photographs, to retrace steps, thought long gone, but not really forgotten.

Many of the events are vivid in my memory, most of them 'firsts'.

First day at the farm, first beating, first day at school, the journey and my arrival. Runaway horses, dead horses, skunks, gophers, porcupines and wolves, they were all part of my life, with a few stroppy mink and marauding racoons thrown in for good measure. Not to forget Indians, Chinamen, Mounties and Beard – you'll have to read further to find out about Beard – But with many photographs, my own recollections and the help of relatives, I've been able to relive my Canadian adventure.

FOREWORD

The Children's Overseas Reception Board (CORB) was set up in June 1940, for the sole purpose of arranging evacuation of children abroad.

Thousands made their applications by post, but on the day the scheme became operative, queues had built up at CORB headquarters, in Berkeley Square, London. It was estimated over 3,000 people were in a queue trying to gain more information. Eventually it became so chaotic the police were called to restore order.

The clerical department was overwhelmed. Their numbers had expanded from thirty on the first day to a staggering 620 within a month, to cope with what staff described as an 'avalanche.' It was estimated that within two weeks of being advertised, they had received an astounding 211,448 applications.

The Government were aghast at what they considered to be a completely hysterical response to the idea of overseas evacuation, in fact the Prime Minister (Winston Churchill) was openly opposed to the plan. The very idea of even contemplating sending children abroad, so incensed him that he directed memos should be sent to all government Heads of Departments, instructing them that drastic action must be taken to put an immediate stop to this defeatist talk. Winston Churchill considered the navy must be used for more vital purposes than escorting ships whose only duty was to ply children overseas.

Only a few months earlier (February 1940) Hitler had ordered a total U-boat blockade of Britain, so you can see the Prime Minister's point. Shortly afterwards defeatist talk became a criminal offence, punishable by imprisonment.

The public was informed that there were insufficient large vessels to protect the ships carrying evacuees and for a while the idea certainly appeared doomed.

But there were many influential people that were adamant the idea should be investigated and exerted constant pressure on as many ministers as possible. It was also obvious to many families that separation was preferable to allowing their children to witness the horrors of war. They thought the risks of travelling were insignificant in comparison and considered their children would be guaranteed a future, so were quite happy to entrust them to half-willing strangers (In my case relatives).

The idea of evacuees was receiving a great deal of publicity in the Canadian press. They made a great play of the 'duty' Canadians owed the British.

Mr Mackenzie King, the Canadian Prime Minister was, like Churchill, completely against the idea. He thought the difficulties would be insuperable and he would not even consider the scheme.

In an atmosphere of chaos and confusion the Government were trying desperately to get the whole idea abandoned, but many members of CORB continued to forge ahead with the scheme, even though they were deliberately flouting government directives.

They sent a letter to all parents whose child/children had been accepted for evacuation overseas. It mentioned that arrangements were to be made for a naval convoy and in the interests of safety they should regard the information as confidential. It read: "You should not discuss this matter even with your neighbours and you should also ask your child/children not to talk about it."

That was a laugh. It was discovered that over half of the evacuees were never even consulted by their parents – me included – I read of one seven-year-old boy who had been called out from his class and put in a waiting ambulance. Inside were his parents with some luggage. They said their goodbyes, climbed out and closed the door. He was taken alone to a nearby railway station to start his 3,000-mile journey.

In June, the last of the British troops were evacuated from the breaches of Dunkirk and Italy declared war on Britain and France, so CORB were even more adamant that the evacuation of children should go ahead. Eventually they won the day and on Sunday 21st July 1940, the first batch of children sailed from Liverpool to Canada and just to prove the gigantic risks involved, U-boats attacked and torpedoed the convoy sinking four of the escort ships. A bitter lesson indeed, but evacuation continued.

All parents were issued with a circular telling them each child should carry a sufficient amount of food and thirst quenching fruit to last for at least twelve hours. No bottles could be carried, but they advised: "It is desirable that each child should take a half-pint carton filled with milk or water; No chocolate should be included. Pack in a small manageable suitcase or attaché case, items that the child may require for three nights (e.g. Identity card, ration cards, sleep clothes, soap, towel, tooth-brush and toothpaste)

There were quite a few children who had insufficient for their needs, so Mr Simon Marks of Marks and Spencer offered to put a stockpile of £700 worth of children's clothing in Glasgow and Liverpool. It was distributed by the W.V.S.

They were not short of volunteers to act as escorts for the children. If they went to Canada they received £5, and while they were waiting for a ship to bring them back to England they were paid expenses of 31p a day.

I was allocated on the batch, which was to travel on the Duchess of York. On our way out, a ship just in front of us was torpedoed and even though there were survivors, the Captain had instructions not to pick them up but to keep going as he had children on board.

On Tuesday the 17th September 1940, the City of Benares was torpedoed. It led to the death of 294, seventy-seven were children. In a cruel twist of fate, those that perished included two youngsters who had previously survived a torpedo attack on another vessel and they'd had to return home, but the parents had no hesitation in sending them out again, convinced this time, they would enjoy a safe passage.

One family lost five of their ten children in the disaster. Only a year later the five brothers, who had stayed at home, survived the complete destruction of their house in an air raid.

The City of Benares had sailed from Liverpool on Friday 13th. Make of that what you will, but those of a superstitious nature made a great deal of it.

A 500lb torpedo had struck the ship. The shock waves reverberated around the world. The headlines proclaimed, 'Murder at sea,' and ' Mass Murder'. It perpetrated even more Nazi outrage, but now parents saw the evacuation of children abroad as an act of defiance against Hitler. As a result, the tragedy proved a great source of anti-nazi propaganda and strengthened the determination to send children to safer climes.

Five days after the sinking the Prime Minister declared the scheme should be temporarily suspended. Frantic talks went on, but the government won the day and publicly suspended the CORB scheme. It was officially announced on the 2nd October, but there were hundreds of children waiting at ports to board ships and they were still arriving from all over Britain. It was complete chaos. Three hundred children had already boarded the

Llandaff Castle bound for South Africa. They spent only one night on board, then they were sent home. Eventually the situation was resolved but no other children were allowed to be evacuated overseas.

CONTENTS

A bit of Collingwood history
Grange Farm and Leross
The journey
A new beginning
Summer 1940
Autumn 1940
Winter 1940/41
My first Christmas
Spring 1941
Summer 1941
Autumn 1941
Winter 1941/42
Spring 1942
Summer 1942
Autumn 1942
Winter 1942/43
Spring 1943
Summer 1943
Autumn 1943
Winter 1943/44
Spring 1944
Summer 1944
Autumn 1944
Winter 1944/45
Spring 1945
Summer 1945
1946
My first love
Art Work
Fifty Years On
Epilogue

A BIT OF COLLINGWOOD HISTORY

My journey would take me to Grange Farm, Leross, Saskatchewan. A wheat farm worked by my mother's cousin, Allan Collingwood.

He had immigrated to Canada with his brothers Herman and Arthur in the early 1900's. This was the time of the Boer war and Canada had flooded Britain with posters advertising '160 acres of virgin prairie land for ten dollars'.

That slogan, plus the tales of Indians and wild game hunting so impressed the brothers they signed up immediately.

They arrived in Saskatchewan in May 1904, convinced that in three years they'd be able to sell their land for thousands and return home.

With the help of two Indian youths, they built a log cabin to live in. Their trade as carpenters came in very useful, not only for their own buildings but they were able to eke out their existence by working as carpenters for a residential Indian school and mission.

It was 1907 before they managed sufficient funds to purchase some horses and machinery and start farming properly. All the settlers helped each other, sharing any implements they could afford.

Crops were good in the first few years, so in 1913, Allan wrote and asked his fiancée Violet to come over and join him.

She arrived at the beginning of June and they were married immediately.

Six years and two children later, Allan's wife became homesick. They were doing reasonably well and Leross was now thriving, but Violet desperately wanted to return to Hull. So in August 1919 they sold up and returned to Yorkshire. But they soon found out they hated the work in Britain and desperately missed the prairies.

After 3 years and another baby, they could stand it no more, so returned in 1922. Brother Herman had already purchased two quarters of land five miles from town.

A house was included in the sale, but it proved unbelievably cold in the harsh prairie winters, especially for the children. During one cold spell they hung a thermometer on the wall near the beds. It registered twenty below zero. Hoar frost hung on the INSIDE walls of the house.

Everyone worked hard and long trying to tame the unbroken and unyielding earth, often with oxen. Rewards were very few.

1926 proved to be absolutely disastrous. It was November before they threshed the harvest and that was in deep snow. It was all far too damp to sell, so by filling sacks with grain, Allan, like all the other farmers, dried as much as possible around the stove in the kitchen.

The telephone was taken out as they could not afford the $12 rental. (about £2.46 a year) Tea was rarely drunk, as it proved too expensive, so everyone drank cocoa at 69 cents a pound.

It was during this difficult period they decided to build another house on the opposite side of the road.

It was completed in January 1928. Trees and bushes made a natural shelter from the harsh winters, protecting the area around the house and farm buildings.

In 1929 Saskatchewan suffered the worst drought in history. Livestock could barely be sustained and many farmers were now nearly destitute. It was ten years before the economy survived this bitter blow.

When the war broke out in 1939, 100,000 had left the drought stricken prairies. Dust storms were also a regular occurrence through the 'Dirty Thirties.'

In 1940 Allan's two sons, Dennis and Harvey joined the armed forces, now the land which had been so painstakingly broken and might now show some recompense for all that back breaking labour, had to be tilled, furrowed and harvested by one man, assisted only occasionally by his daughter Mary – His wife Violet would not even collect the eggs and they were now to be joined by a small six-year-old city girl from England.

GRANGE FARM

It was situated just over four miles from Leross and two miles from Ravine School.

Most of the buildings were made from hewn logs, liberally coated with a mixture of mud, dung and straw. The biffy was a small wooden shed about one hundred yards from the house. A wooden seat was placed strategically over a deep hole. When that became full, the shed was moved to another location and the hole covered over.

They had about thirty head of cattle, four horses, several pigs, twenty mink, a hundred or so chickens, enough turkeys to make some very nice dinners, a motley collection of felines and a dog called Buster.

The main crops were wheat, oats and barley. Alfalfa was sown as nutritious food for the animals. The farm was completely self-sufficient.

LEROSS

This was the small town in Saskatchewan that for five years was to be the nearest point of civilisation for me.

Indians, Blackfoot, Cree and Metis inhabited the area until the early 1900's when the first settlers arrived, which included Allan, Herman and Arthur Collingwood.

They lived happily with the local Indians, who soon taught them how to build shelters from the materials on hand.

By 1906, they decided to build a school for the 18 or so children in the area.

It was 1908 before the Pacific Railway reached that far into the prairies, with grain elevators following three years later.

Moving from the West, all the towns were named in alphabetical order. The name often taken from a member of the gang, working hard to bring civilisation to the settlers. Kelliher had just been named and when the railroad arrived in town it had to begin with an L. They settled on the boss of the rail gang, a Mr L. E. Ross

By the thirties, one or two of the farmers were getting motorised transport, plus of course trucks that brought supplies. Walter Sotski decided to open a service station. No one had electricity, so he ran his own power plant from a 32-volt generator, run by a water-cooled engine. It had two gas pumps, one bowl held white gas, one red (Ethyol) each one had to be pumped by hand and each bowl held ten gallons of gasoline.

Elevators dominated the Leross skyline. All the farmers took their wheat to town in wagons, pulled by strong teams. They then went into a drive through shed, which housed the public weigh scale.

An agent graded it, a price would be negotiated, determined by the appearance and plumpness of the kernel and its weight. The railcars were then loaded with the grain from the wagons by hand scoops. These crops were shipped to all corners of the globe, including Ranks flourmill in Yorkshire, near the Collingwood brother's home in England. Elevators were placed eight to eleven miles mile apart, always on the side of rail tracks as this was considered an acceptable distance for a horse to pull the heavy wagons.

THE JOURNEY

From the Land of Green Ginger.
1940

The atmosphere was decidedly odd. My brother had been shunted off to Auntie Ronnies and my mother was windmilling around the house, checking gas, closing windows and locking doors. I'd never seen her in such a dither.

"I've put some things on your bed, go upstairs and put them on."

"Is it Sunday?"

"Of course it's not Sunday."

"Why do I have to put me best things on then?"

"Because I said so, now go and get dressed."

New frock, socks, shoes and knickers. This must be something special.

"Are you going to be up there all day?"

In a flurry of pearl buttons and shoe buckles, I bounded down the stairs.

"Can I go to Auntie Ronnies?"

"No, you can't."

"Am I 'aving me picture took?"

"Picture? Why should you be 'aving your picture took?"

"'Cos you've made me wear me best things."

"Will you stop going on. You are not 'aving your picture took and that's that."

She held out a new red coat.

"Can't I wear me white cardi.?"

"No, you can't."

"But I like it."

"I said NO."

I remember having my picture taken in that cardigan. Near the studio, was a narrow, cobbled street, called The Land of Green Ginger. It boasts the smallest window in the world.

Mum's voice interrupted my reverie.

"Oh, and go to the lav. before we go."

Go! Go where?

In her mood, I thought I'd better not ask.

I padded across the stone scullery floor, passing the gas cooker and the wash boiler in the corner, solid against the green distempered walls.

I thought it was Monday, but Monday was always washday.

By 7am the coal burning copper would be burning furiously. Clothes and bed linen would have been dumped into the bubbling water. After boiling, wooden tongs lifted the heavy sodden garments into a metal dolly tub, cascading scalding water all over the floor. Then they were twisted around with a wooden dolly stick or posher. A tangled saturated heap would then be heaved into the large, stone sink adding a bag of dolly blue and some cold water starch, after kneading and pummelling them into submission, they'd be hand wrung into the waiting tin bath below.

At weekends this doubled as a bath. One lot of water for all of us. Last in ended up greyer than when they started.

I stepped out into the back yard and by stretching on my tiptoes, could just reach the rusty sneck on the lavatory door.

While sitting on the cracked wooden seat, I noticed, dangling from the nail embedded in the crumbling brickwork, just one square of newspaper left on the twine. I must cut some more up when I returned.

"Are you going to be in there all day? If you don't hurry up we'll be late."

Late! Late for what?

Mum was already in the backyard, carrying an old, brown suitcase and clutching a parcel wrapped with string and a paper bag. She handed me the bag. "There, you can carry that."

Before I had time to peek inside she'd grabbed my hand and was leading me swiftly down the back passage and into the street, walking past rows of undistinguished, anonymous houses.

We stopped at the sweet shop on the corner. I was told I could choose two of anything I wanted. Wow! Sherbert Suckers? When my brother sucked through the hollow liquorice straw, he could make froth come out of his nose. Or maybe a Liquorice Shoelace? These were great fun. After uncoiling them you would skip around with black strips dangling from your mouth, sucking it up inch by inch. But I loved gobstoppers. They lasted for days. You kept pulling it out of your mouth to see how big it was. A toffee lollipop dipped in icing sugar? Or maybe a pennyworth of broken toffee. Decision time. My choice? A cinnamon stick and a sherbet sucker.

I remembered to say please and thank you, because the grumpy man behind the counter wouldn't serve you if you didn't, also I'd get a reminder from Mum - a wallop around the ear.

We turned the corner and walked briskly past the church, then I saw Dad with his bike, standing next to a trolley stop sign.

He grinned broadly, tipping his flat cap to the back of his fair curly hair. Taking the suitcase from mum he placed it on the handlebars, then swinging a leg over the saddle, gave a cheery wave and rode off. Mum took the paper bag from me.

Ding! Ding! Startled, I jumped round as a trolley bus drew alongside.

We climbed on. Still not a word had been spoken.

Ding! Ding! We were off. I could see my Dad with his heavy black boots, pedalling furiously.

I'd never been on a trolley before. We usually walked everywhere.

I remember thinking, it was a bit like sitting in a pot of maggots. Pale people, shuffling around. Always on the move.

Dad was already waiting when we arrived in the city centre. We all walked to the rail station, Mum tightly clutching my hand and Dad balancing the brown case still perched on the handlebars.

It was a confusion of hustle and bustle.

Propping his bike against a newspaper kiosk, Dad disappeared, leaving us to watch the discordant throng.

When he returned, mum, who still had not spoken a word, suddenly burst into tears. Dad knelt down beside me.

"Now, you are going to be a good girl aren't you?"

Why was it so important?

His rough hand gripped mine and with Mum still sniffing loudly, we headed for the barrier. Clouds of pervasive steam enveloped the travellers.

I couldn't believe it. We were going on a train.   I'd never been on a train.   'Oh', I thought, 'Nonnie will be furious.' But why hadn't they brought my brother as well?   Never mind, I could tell him all about it later.

A carriage was selected. A large, florid lady with flat feet stood by the window.

My parents began talking to her. The lady turned, looked at me quizzically and then smiled. I decided I liked her and smiled back.

The case and the parcel were lifted onto an overhead rack, the paper bag was placed on a seat. Both parents kissed me on the top of my head and again I was told: "Be a good girl," followed by: "That lady will look after you."

Why should this lady look after me. Why didn't Mum and Dad want to stay on the train with me?

As they were stepping from the carriage, Mum turned and said: "Oh, by the way, there's something to eat and drink in your bag." She turned and walked briskly away.

Little did I know that five years would elapse before I set eyes on my brother, parents or the Land Of Green Ginger again.

It was July 1940 and the battle which was to be fought throughout Europe, had already begun.

The first time the sirens pierced our slumbers, Mum decided we should all hide under the stairs, with the perception that, whenever you saw a ruined house, the stairs were usually intact!

Two adults, two children, coats, shoes, brooms, three tins of lime green distemper, old curtains, football boots and a cricket bat were crammed in there for nearly two hours. Well, as they say, it seemed a good idea at the time.

After that it was the shelter in a nearby schoolyard. It had bunks for the children to sleep in, but we were often outside playing, usually marbles or hopscotch, that is until the ominous drone of a bomber and distant gunfire could be heard, then we were quickly ushered inside. Except on the first big raid. They hadn't had time to put a roof on! But on subsequent raids, from the safety of the completed shelter, we watched in amazement as Britain and Germany locked horns. Searchlight beams scanned the heavens, illuminating the lumbering barrage balloons drifting in the midnight sky.

As a large and important port, Hull was proving to be a prime target, so my parents made a momentous decision. Evacuation. I was never warned my life was about to be turned upside down, because at six years of age, they decided I was too young to understand. "Be a good girl," was considered enough warning for a journey to a strange land and anonymous strangers.

I was ushered halfway around the world like a walking parcel, with only a luggage label attached to my lapel with a large nappy pin, for identification.

My smiling lady escorted me off the train, carrying my suitcase and parcel. Friendly faces were everywhere. The label was inspected, then my hand firmly grasped and I was led to a large room, packed with children. A cacophony of sound greeted me. I was placed at the end of a bawling queue of assorted youngsters. I soon found out why. Everyone was being vaccinated.

Poor, bewildered bairns were then herded into smaller rooms, to be prodded and inspected by ladies in white coats. We were even checked for lice.

I remember I got them once. Mum put a sheet of newspaper on the linoleum and then made me kneel on the floor, combing my hair over it. The ticks leapt off the paper with the velocity of a bullet. I was well impressed – Mother was not!

At the annual Hull fair, one of my favourite side-shows was the flea-circus. You could see them chariot racing, high wire walking and swinging on a flying trapeze. Fascinating, and here was my mother splatting them all over the floor.

After all the checks, we were given orange juice and a biscuit. I had an apple left in my bag, but I thought I'd keep it.

I watched as labels were inspected and youngsters led away, never to return.

My wooden bench was getting increasingly uncomfortable. I thought about my Uncle Ted and Auntie Kath, who for as treat, only two days previously, had taken my brother and me to the East Coast resort of Withernsea. We travelled in the little sidecar of his beloved motor bike.

On the beach we made sand castles, proudly sticking little Union Jacks on the turrets.

We laughed at the antics of Punch and Judy and paddled in the cold North Sea.

I was thinking about eating my apple when another smiling lady approached me. Now it was my turn. I was led to another train and allowed to sit next to the window and watch the billowing smoke drift by. I fervently wished my brother could be with me. It was so exciting. An eruption of explosive steam heralded our arrival and widely contrasting children spilled out onto the platform to be met by more smiling ladies. Lines of silent youngsters were ushered through the station to be herded onto busses.

Recently I found out that all station signs were removed during the war. I bet that caused problems.

Overnight was to be spent in a schoolroom. We were pointed in the direction of a mattress and one hairy, grey blanket, which tickled. "After you've got washed (in cold water, in small wash-basins) put your clothes under your head for a pillow and your gas-masks at your feet."

We settled uneasily in these strange surroundings. Many were crying.

Next morning we were all given a drink of milk and hustled out of the school.

After a short coach trip we were spilling out into another strange location. The air was brisk and we could see a large expanse of water and we were met by a plethora of smiling sailors. All ready to escort us onto the Duchess of York.

"Come on Princess, up you go."

I looked up at the steep gangplank and hesitated.

"Don't worry," said a tall, genial sailor. I liked him. He had fair, curly hair just like my dad's. Hands reached under my arms and I was casually swung onto his shoulders. We threaded our way through a torrent of people, up stairs, along corridors and through innumerable doors.

At last I was deposited in a small, four-berth cabin, already occupied by a dark forbidding lady and a dumpling of a girl with pigtails.

We were soon joined by a sturdy ten year-old, wearing thick, heavy glasses, black lace-up boots and green woollen mittens.

We were shown how to put on our life jackets and were told they had to be worn night and day.

After about an hour, the lady escorted us to the deck. The ship was starting to move. Lots of people were on the quayside and they started singing, 'There'll always be an England,' they were soon joined by everyone on board. People were leant over the rail frantically waving and singing.

My sailor friend said he would look out for me. He did, he was there every time we had to practise climbing into the lifeboats – which was daily. He once gave me an orange.

We'd only been at sea a day or so when U-boats torpedoed a ship just ahead of us. It was sunk and although there were survivors, the captain had instructions to keep going as he had children on board.

They used to organise talent contests and boxing matches, with biscuits as a prize. There were several lectures on Canada. I particularly liked the one about birds. We also had the board games, ludo, snakes and ladders and draughts to play with.

I was talked to, cuddled, dangled, educated, enlightened, interviewed and amused. Some days it was my turn to entertain. Well I had had three tap dancing lessons! I performed my 'turn' under the barrels of anti-aircraft guns which were primed and ready for action and manned twenty-four hours a day.

A flurry of emotional ladies met us when we disembarked in Halifax, Nova Scotia. I always understood we landed in Montreal, but research showed it was Nova Scotia.

I was led to yet another train and placed in a compartment. My battered suitcase beside me and my name and forwarding address now tied on a piece of string round my neck.

"Hello."

I was confronted by a tall, heavily built porter. Immaculate uniform with gleaming buttons, matching his sunshine smile.

I couldn't speak. My eyes voyaged over his face. He was black!

I thought everyone in the world was white.

"Are you hungry?" he enquired.

I nodded. He held out his hand. I rose, clasped his little finger and trustingly followed him to the restaurant car.

He seated me next to a lady with a dead animal draped around her shoulders and a silly, blue hat perched on top of her coal, black hair, scraped back into an untidy bun. Her thin, bespectacled son wore a tie the colour of mushy peas.

They asked me lots of questions, most of which I couldn't answer, then told me they had three dogs. Three! We didn't even have one.

I once determinedly pulled a reluctant stray all the way from school and insisted; "But mum, it followed me all the way home." My pleas fell on deaf ears, I was despatched to the nearby police station to hand in my new-found friend.

I persistently lugged unsuspecting animals home, but it never worked. Then I had a brainwave. Mum said we couldn't have a dog, she never said anything about a cat! With great optimism I set forth. The ones I did manage to catch were not very impressed by me sticking them inside my coat so I soon became disillusioned and gave up the idea of a pet.

But back to the meal, here I was perfectly happy to be sat with two perfect strangers – well maybe not perfect – in a strange land.

After I'd eaten, I was collected by my new friend, who escorted to my sleeping quarters. They were in a compartment for eight. He lifted me onto an upper berth, telling me he would watch over me all night, then pulling the curtains across, left me to sleep.

He became my favourite person. I followed him everywhere. I was enjoying every minute.

On the third day, the train shuddered to a halt at Leross, a small prairie town, in Saskatchewan. Walter effortlessly lifted me onto the wooden platform, setting my case beside me.

I stood perplexed. Why had he deposited me here? I looked up. Solemnly heading towards me was a gaunt unshaven man with an air of isolation about him and an erect, unsmiling lady, an incongruous elegance surrounding her in a land of billowing wheat.

I heard a shrill whistle. My friend had gone.

"I'm Auntie Vi. and that's Uncle Allan," and without further ado my case was picked up and they walked towards a horse and buggy, which was standing in the shadow of a giant grain elevator. I was obviously expected to follow.

This was a rather alarming turn of events. I wasn't sure I wanted them to be my auntie and uncle.

Having been brought up in a noisy dirty city, I didn't think much to being catapulted into a strange and silent land.

The air hung heavy and insects droned in the prairie heat. No horizon could be identified, it just went on forever.

My woollen coat was heavy and uncomfortable. I felt like a detached spectator, being bumped and jostled as the horse gathered speed along the dusty, rutted road. I burst into tears. The lady patted my hand.

The buggy drew up outside a wooden house in the middle of a field.

We pushed through a wire-meshed door. Didn't they have wooden ones? Inside, were unfamiliar things. What was that black, round, tubby thing in the middle of the room?

A tall, slim, porcelain figure, with rich brown hair and luminous dark eyes came and shook my hand. "Hello, I'm Mary." I said nothing. Nobody had ever shaken my hand before.

She asked if I wanted anything to eat. I shook my head. I just wanted to go home. They motioned me to sit on a bench at a scrubbed, wooden table. I noticed there were several sticky fly-papers dangling from the ceiling. They seemed to have a more varied selection of winged insects than we did at home. Uncle Allen took my suitcase up the stairs.

"Right," said Mary, "I expect you're tired, so we'd better get you ready for bed."

Aunt Violet, brought in an old tin bucket, while Mary asked to me to undress. They washed my hands, face and neck, then told me to put on my pyjamas.

"Say goodnight," said Mary. I did. "Good," she nodded, "Now I'll show you your bedroom." I padded quietly after her.

A single iron bedstead, covered with a patchwork quilt and a home-made wooden chest of drawers, were set against the timber lined walls.

"There's a potty under the bed." said Mary, then turned on her heel, shutting the door behind her.

The footsteps echoed as they receded down the bare wooden stairs.

I climbed into bed. My eyes voyaged endlessly over the knots in the wood, fashioning them into family faces.

Imagination seethed in the uneasiness of twilight.

A blood-curdling howl, shattered my reverie, startled I dived under the bedclothes and cried myself to sleep. It was a restless sleep. I had a dream, come nightmare, which I remember with great clarity. My body could enlarge or diminish at will. I seemed to be enveloped in the fleshpots of my mind, but sometimes imagination exceeded willpower and like a balloon, I would expand to giant proportions, completely filling the room. I could watch myself in almost infinitesimal proportions standing in the centre of this monstrous flesh existence. But I felt trapped and afraid. I was swallowing myself. There was no escape. 'Make yourself smaller Dorothea. Quick, before you're swallowed up.'

'No,' said the voice, 'You'll be lost forever.'

'I wont, I wont. Please stop now! Please, please bring me back, I don't want to be swallowed, slowly or quickly.'

The fleshy bubble started to collapse around me and I slowly returned to normality.

I lay staring at the wooden ceiling, streaked with the silver moonlight, but the 'voice' hadn't finished. 'Don't close your eyes Dorothea, you can still be swallowed up.'

I forced my eyes to stare straight ahead, my body rigid, not daring to move a muscle.

Then I thought it safe to try and close my eyes … very slowly … very, very slowly. No! NO! That's too fast …. There's that's better. Now try again.

Oh, dear I can still see the moon through my closed lids. My flesh balloon's gone … I think. My eyes are heavy. I wonder if the clouds are still scudding across the sky. I'll look in a minute … In a min–in a… in…

The end of a journey, but the birth of an extraordinary and remarkable life.

Day out at Withernsea with brother Norris

A row of anonymous houses

Paragon Station Hull

Allan and Buster

Violet

Mary

Grange Farm house

A NEW BEGINNING

SUMMER 1940

I lay there watching the first fingers of daylight filter through my small window. See, it was my window already. The pale blush washed the bare room of nightmares. A myriad of birdsong tumbled around my gold streaked dawn.

Another unfamiliar sound splintered my abstract thoughts, not quite as fearsome as the night before but I still felt apprehensive. It was loud and boastful. The perfect voice for the swaggering cockerel.

I heard footsteps. The door opened and a face peeped around the edge. It was the dark haired lady. She smiled. "Hello, how are you this morning?"

I smiled back.

"Come on," she said, "Shall we get dressed?"

But she was already dressed! Anyway WE got dressed and went downstairs.

The stairs led directly onto small, sparsely furnished room and an even smaller kitchen beyond. A crisp blue gingham curtain fluttered in the morning breeze. Dominating the room was a black, pot-bellied stove, with a heavy black pipe bending and curling through the wooden ceiling.

I could see Auntie Vi. and Uncle Allan sitting at a scrubbed wooden table in the kitchen. Food and utensils were neatly stacked on nearby shelves. Aunti Vi. bade me to sit beside her on a long bench.

"Would you like some corn-on-the-cob for breakfast?" she asked.

"No, thank you."

"Some pancakes then?"

"No thank you."

"I'm sure you'd like some bacon and eggs."

Now we were on familiar territory. But for breakfast! At home that was our main meal and then only once a week. I decided I'd pass.

"No thank you."

Desperation was beginning to set in, so Mary had a go.

"How about some bread and syrup?"

"No thank you."

Despairing glances were passed around.

"Bread and jam?"

"Oh yes. Please. That's my favourite."

Every morning I ate bread and jam for breakfast. On the sixth day Auntie Vi had a brainwave. She substituted the word syrup for treacle.

I clapped my hands gleefully. "Yes, please. Treacle's my very, very favourite."

Everyone laughed uproariously. We were all sharing a special moment together. I felt completely at ease. I was home.

For the first few weeks I padded around after Mary, helping with the daily chores. It took only a short while before I was feeding the chickens, collecting eggs and drawing water from the well on my own. I even helped in churning butter.

I would be up at 6.30am and after a hearty breakfast – including corn-on the-cob – I would pick up a galvanised pail and carefully check out the nests in the hen coops – notice I used the word pail? It didn't take long did it?

34

After depositing the eggs, still warm and covered in thistledown in the house, I'd be off to help feed the mink. They were kept in runs, suspended about three feet above the ground. At feeding time I would be despatched along the cages, which was covered by chicken wire and by running my finger along the bottom wire, I would alert them to breakfast. Many a time my chubby index would get caught in the wire, but it was soon pulled out and I galloped on.

Except once! I was helping Dennis, their son, who was home on leave from the air-force, when my finger got stuck, but this time the mink was already in the run. He couldn't believe his luck when he saw this tasty pink digit waving at him. He pounced. I screamed

The mink, momentarily distracted by the explosion of noise, relinquished his grip. I pulled free. Dennis grabbed me under the arms and unceremoniously swung me onto his shoulders. Blood was pouring from the wound as he raced to the house. My finger was placed in a bowl of salted water, then while I was held very firmly, iodine was poured over the jagged gash. My finger was bound tightly and I was told to sit still and stop crying.

I did. They expected immediate obedience.

I was always apprehensive that any punishment meted out would not be very pleasant and I had no intention of finding out. After tending the wound, they left me. A farm is a very busy place and not much time was left over for loving, so I sat very still and very uncomfortably on a small three-legged stool not daring to move.

I still have the scar to this day.

Next day although the finger was very sore and still bleeding slightly, I felt fine and had no hesitation in returning to my mink round.

In the afternoon I was asked to assist in taking a long wooden box to the mink runs.

With a gloved hand, a mink was taken from the run and placed in the box. After a while it was taken out, dead. Five or six mink were despatched in the same way, but at the time didn't know what they were doing to the animals. I found out later that exhaust fumes from the thresher engine gassed them. The following year Uncle Allan bought some cyanide shavings. These were deposited in a tray in the bottom of the box, which was completely air-proof.

Uncle Allan and Dennis carried the dead animals to a small shed, where they proceeded to skin them. Taking care not to make mark or tear in the prized pelts.
I watched fascinated as the pale flesh was revealed, without a drop of blood being seen. The luxurious, velvety furs were then spread-eagled along the walls of the shed and left to dry. It was explained to me that by selling the pelts, it would pay for all the provisions and essentials for the smooth running of the farm.
I looked in daily to see the progress and watched in fascination as the taut pelts dried naturally. The fur gently curling around the edges as the skins retracted.

Dennis had returned to his squadron and I was helping Uncle Allan in the barn.
"The pelts are ready now, so would you like to come into Leross with me and meet a few people?"
"Yes please."
Town consisted of a collection of wooden buildings and a wooden sidewalk along one side, complete with a hitch rail for the horses. The livery stable was the only building to wear any paint. It was bright red, like a spit, polished apple.

We first hitched the buggy outside a Chinese immigrant's shop, Charlie Limm.
It had originally been the local hotel, with the only liquor licence in the area. Uncle Allan's brothers, Herman and Arthur built it in 1912. It was more than adequate for the local drinking

habits. Four years later the temperance movement succeeded in closing all the bars in the country but the farmers soon found other ways of imbibing. (Which is well documented in my book Beyond the Brave) The building then became a poolroom. This was bought by Charlie when he landed in Leross while labouring to lay the railroad across Canada - The workforce was predominately Chinese - Like many before him, Charlie Limm skipped the gangs and settled down.

We pushed through the mosquito door and after the bright sunlight, it looked rather dim and dingy. What a disappointment. Uncle Allan said his niece Marion thought it was magical. Then I saw the shafts of light filtering through the windows, like a fairy-tale staircase. All along one side from floor to ceiling, were shelves of material. From denim and serge, to bolts of shimmering satin and fresh gingham, exploding in a cascade of colour in the dancing sunbeams. Every inch of one wall was covered with a great variety of goods and the floor was littered with barrels and boxes filled to overflowing. I could see pickled herring, cheddar cheese, lard, cookies, horse collars, harness, kerosene, lamps, sugar and candles. Marion was right. It was magical.

A diminutive, genial man leant over the counter.

" 'ello Allan, oo dis den?"

"Dot, she's from England and is staying with us for a while."

He beamed. "You like candy?"

I nodded. He came round from behind the counter and kneeling down handed me a striped candy -stick.

Why did he kneel down? He was only a titch, but he had the most extraordinary smile. It seemed to fill his whole face. His ears wiggled when he talked and his eyes disappeared completely.

He returned behind the counter.

"Right, Allan, what you want today den?"

Allan retrieved a shopping list from his pocket. Suddenly we noticed a shadowy figure stood in the semi-darkness at the far side of the store. He made his way forward, leaning heavily on two crutches. The pressure he used to help him walk with the crutches, had given him the most extraordinary muscular arms, tanned to a deep mahogany brown. He was swearing profusely, as if he was angry at some unseen force. The wind had tousled his thick black hair. I wasn't so sure about this strange individual, so I quickly stepped behind Uncle Allen. Not a word was spoken, just a cursory nod and he was gone. His crutches thudding rhythmically on the wooden sidewalk.

"That was Willy," explained Uncle Allen. "And he had an accident some years ago."

"You tell little lady story." Mr Limm pointed excitedly at me. "He been in town all day drinking and den climb on buckboard to go home. His 'osses, they always knew when he drunk. In't that right Allan?"

"That's right Charlie."

"He always drunk. Every day he get drunk. I'n't dat right Allan?"

"Wouldn't argue with that."

"You tell 'er Allan, you tell 'er."

A quiet smile crossed Uncle Allan's face as he took up the story.

"Well as soon as he climbed onto the buckboard the horses started running away."

Charlie started gesticulating wildly. "Dem not 'osses. Dem bronco's. Dey real wild 'osses." He leant conspiritorily over the counter. "Dem white bronco's and dey run away all right. Okay Allan, now you tell little lady what 'appen when dey run away and Willy, he yell whoa, whoa, as loud as 'e can. It velly loud. Everybody hear."

Uncle Allan smiled at the vociferous Chinaman knowing he would carry on. He did.

"But 'osses took not bit of blinded notice. Go on tell 'er what 'appened when dey turn round in street. You tell. I see it little lady, I see it."

"So you did Charlie, so you did."

38

"'e was thrown from the buckboard. Oohh, it was terrible, 'e broke both 'is legs, didn't 'e Allan?"

"Yes, it was very sad."

"Yes, it sad. Him very sad man." Muttered Mr Limm. Then abruptly looked at Uncle Allan and asked, "Yes, what you want den?"

Uncle Allan consulted his list. "Just some sugar, lard and blocks of salt for the cattle."

We collected the goods and after putting them in the back of the buggy, headed for Hall's store with the pelts. Above the door hung a sign, which read: "I am H. M. Hall, not the Bank of Montreal, so don't ask for credit."

This was even better than Mr Limms. I could see hammers, nails, shells, horse collars, buckles, even knives and pocket watches. There was a giant pot bellied stove in the centre.

There were already three farmers in there showing off weasels, wolves, rabbits, fox and mink. Haggling and bargaining filled the air, pelts of every size, shape and colour were hung in great swathes from the ceiling. Without exception farmers challenged the price offered, it was always too low and the price his neighbour received was always far, far too high.

Uncle Allen introduced me to everyone. They all patted my head, then started haggling again. After deciding on a reasonable price for the mink he turned to Mr Hall, a solid, ruddy-faced individual, with a great shock of silver hair.

"Got a favour to ask Hally,"

"Yep, just ask"

"The young 'un here. Will you keep an eye on her? I've heard Charlie Cockle has some young horses in the auction and I'd like to have a look."

"Yep, you get on to the sale, I'll see she's looked after."

He brought a small stool used for reaching top shelves.

"There you, you can sit on my special stool."

The shop was a veritable treasure trove. He sold everything from bullets to barbed wire and pocket watches to shovels.

As I was exploring the myriad of small drawers there was a commotion outside, we both rushed onto the street to see what was happening. A group of horses were galloping towards the auctioneers, one with a ladder around its neck! Suddenly a voice yelled, "That's my bloody ladder. Grab 'em quick."

In minutes farmers had climbed aboard a horse or leapt in a buggy and were giving chase. The auction had been forgotten. We watched as the 'posse' disappeared up the street after them, then returned inside. I was having a wonderful time ferreting around in some barrels. Eventually the horses were herded back, none the worse for wear. The ladder had lost a few rungs but that was about all. Uncle Allan didn't buy a horse but returned to Mr Halls and bought some barbed wire and nails. Then we headed back to Grange Farm.

In the corral with Buster

Belle

With Dennis, Buster and farmcat

Dennis

This is "H.M. Hall, not the bank of Montreal!"

Pelts in Mr Hall's Shop

AUTUMN 1940

I was now feeling completely at home and without any prompting I began calling Uncle Allan Pops, and Auntie Vi. became Auntie Mum.

It was late summer with the sun dismally trying to find a way through the threatening clouds – Chickens were perched in the trees ready for the long night, appearing almost luminous as they settled in the branches away from predators.

Much had to be done to prepare for winter. It was not unusual in the prairies for a farm to be completely snowed up for up to five months, so provisions had to be adequate for animals as well as humans. I was speechless when I saw whole sides of beef and pork, salted and hung up in an outside shed in preparation for our enforced isolation.

Although stock was regularly killed, I'd never seen anything untoward – yet.

Livestock was corralled beside their respective barns and the hens would have to forsake their freedom and sleep in their coops. - Thinking about it, I expect that's where the saying 'cooped up' originated – Their winter quarters was just a long low shed of rough hewn logs, which had been lathered with a mud, straw and dung compound.

Snow started falling in mid-September, transforming the trees into sugar concoctions, by the last week in October it was six-foot deep and branches were bent low with the heavy snow. It was at this point we had to shovel snow over the coops. Further falls obliterated them completely, ensuring they became underground bunkers, virtually invisible except for the path which was dug out daily and a small area for them to come out and have a good old 'scrat'

I spent quite a lot of time looking through my bedroom window, watching herds of deer foraging for food and I soon knew when their enemies the wolf and coyote were in the vicinity, as they beat a hasty retreat. These scavengers travelled in marauding packs and they could clearly be seen, upturned faces silhouetted in the bright moonlight, as they emitted fearsome howls which echoed around the night..

Darkness has never held any terrors for me – except once.

I had been asked to go to the barn to check some heifers. I made my way through a small wooded area, the branches exploding darkly overhead, as my oil-lamp flickering uncertainly in the cold night air casting eerie shadows along the winding path. All was well with the beasts, so I headed back. Suddenly from behind me came a shrill scream, I turned and from the cavern of moonlight and shadows, a shrieking apparition, was heading straight towards me.

Terror momentarily rooted me to the spot, but only momentarily. Whirling around I raced towards the safety of the house, the lamp now extinguished with the ferocious swinging. I burst through the door and rushed to Mary, who was sat quietly doing some needlework.

"It got me, it nearly got me." I announced breathlessly.

I clung to her skirt, shaking with fright. She didn't seem the slightest bit interested. And with an exasperated sigh said: "Oh, for heaven's sake, there's nothing to be frightened of. It'll have been that silly old barn owl."

"It wasn't an owl. It wasn't 'onest. This was more giantist than an owl."

Of this I was absolutely convinced.

"Well it was the old barn owl and you're being a silly girl. You're making a fuss over nothing."

She carried on with her needlework.

Pops and Auntie Mum were also in the room but said nothing, in fact they never even looked up.

"Anyway it's about time you got ready for bed."

I started for the door.

"Not immediately," she said sharply. "We haven't had bible reading yet."

I obediently sat at the table. Needlework was carefully placed on the table and Auntie Mum reached for the heavy old bible, which was lying on a lace doily on the top of a heavy chest of drawers. Five minutes later I was dismissed and it was upstairs to bed.

As I snuggled up into the security of my own little world, I would never admit to being afraid again.

Only an old barn owl indeed. At that speed it certainly wasn't old!

I loved it when the heavy snows came, I spent an inordinate amount of time building igloos. Long ones, short ones, round ones, square ones, with tunnels, without tunnels, with windows, without windows. My first one boasted a liberal coating of straw on the floor and two small windows, it even had two snow chairs!

Buster the dog had one, so had the cats, but they were not enamoured when I lugged them from a cosy hayloft, only to stuff them in a freezing igloo. Buster was quite content to cuddle up to me, but only for a few minutes at a time.

I built a whole family of snowmen. I rolled a snowball down the hill, but they collected so much snow on the way down, they were too big to push back up to the top, so they were left there, guarding the field. Rolling from the bottom up reduced the size, so I ended up with an army of children watching over the igloo estate. I even fashioned cats, dogs and horses. Manes and tails were constructed from twigs and hay. The next morning I rushed out to find we'd had another heavy snowstorm. My igloo now had two feet of snow – inside. So I built another, but this time I left out the windows and bunged up the entrance with a huge snowball. All my snow people were now unrecognisable and appeared as huge protuberances pushing up through the snow.

MY FIRST CHRISTMAS

I peeped outside onto a cold, bright, silent world. I had been promised a trip to the Christmas school concert, five miles away, if the weather held.

"Nice and crisp out there,' said a voice behind me. 'Looks like we'll be able to make the concert after all.'

I clapped my hands in delight. Pops allowed himself a slight smile.

We set off in the early afternoon, our sleigh bumping over the rutted snow. After settling Belle, our shaggy grey mare, in the livery stable we headed for the schoolhouse. Inside, I was introduced to many of our neighbours, who like us had travelled several miles in their home-made sleighs.

The inviting nature of the prairie settlers was evident as they greeted me for the first time. Most patted me on the head like a small puppy. I felt warm and loved.

I noticed all the desks were lined up against the wall with their lids up and nearly everyone had a baby inside. One bellowing infant was being changed and as we passed it, it seemed to explode. Quite the most spectacular poohing session I'd ever seen.

When everyone had settled in their seats, a large, balding man with a round, flushed face and great bushy side-whiskers, came to the front and announced: 'We will start the evening by singing 'O'Canada,' followed by 'Away in a Manager.'

The piano introduction began and everyone sang lustily. I didn't know either of them but I pretended I did. The lady stood next to Auntie Mum made people giggle because her singing was so loud she sounded like a bellowing cow.

The carol was followed by a poem, recited by a small girl with long golden plaits and a face as speckled as a bird's egg. Then a round boy in overalls and a screwed up sort of face, recited a poem about winter. When we all clapped he started again, but a long, thin man with scuttling eyebrows, tucked him under his arm and strode off.

Suddenly there was a commotion to our left. A cat, which had obviously crept in to escape from the icy blasts, had settled down in a desk, but was now being unceremoniously dumped back outside, except it escaped the clutches of its captor and trampolined across the comatose babies, culminating in one gigantic leap onto the rafters above. There it perched, glaring balefully at the assembled throng. It was decided it should be left.

Next a chunky boy, called George, stood up and sang 'When Father Papered the Parlour.' Well he shouted really, but I didn't pay much attention, as I couldn't take my eyes off his wild ginger hair. It sprouted alarmingly from all angles like little scrubbing brushes.

Miss Vaughn, the teacher told us that the concert would conclude by a performance by the over twelve's, and it would be a shadow play.

A large white sheet was stretched across the stage and a lamp lowered so the silhouettes were lifelike. Anne Katelnikof stood at the side of the stage and said: 'I'm afraid there has been an accident and you are about to see the scene in the operating theatre.' She then disappeared behind the sheet.

We watched as the shadow of a moaning patient with a crushed leg was placed on the operating table. Doctors and nurses could be seen examining him. A doctor declared, 'There's nothing we can do. The leg will have to be cut off.' I wasn't sure about this. I'd never seen a leg sawn off before. The doctor issued instructions. 'Chloroform the patient.' The wild moaning coming from the man on the operating table slowly subsided.

'Saw,' commanded a shadowy figure. The patient gave a final gasp. Ooh's and aahh's filled the air. I held my breath. We saw the outline of a saw as it was handed to the doctor. You could have heard a pin drop. Then we all heard the terrible fou-ba-fou-ba as the saw tore through the leg. The patient started to moan. Some children in front tried to peep under the sheet but they were quickly shooed back to their seats. I was peeping through my fingers. Finally we heard a dull thud as the severed limb dropped to the floor. The patient gave a long sigh. The doctor came to the front of the white sheet and proclaimed: 'The operation was a huge success and I guarantee he'll be up and about with a wooden leg in no time.'

The applause was thunderous. I asked Pops what they did with the blood, but he told me not to worry, as there wouldn't have been much. 'There was,' I told him, 'I saw it oozing out of his leg,' but before he could answer, the sound of sleigh bells was heard outside. A loud ho-ho-ho and in strode Kris Kringle, his red suit trimmed with real fur and a large sack tossed over his shoulders. Inside was a present for every child. I received an orange and a be-ribbonned candy stick. After waving him goodbye, we muffled up against the biting cold and with every baby accounted for we all headed home. Pops said one year a baby had got left behind. 'I don't wonder it doesn't happen more often,' muttered Auntie Mum, 'When you've got a brood of eleven or twelve offspring, it must be easy to miss a body or two.'

I sat snug in the sleigh between the two grown-ups, our legs covered by a wolfskin fur and looked up at the sky. It was studded with a million diamonds and tomorrow was Christmas day.

The family was already in the kitchen when I ran downstairs. 'Doesn't look like he's been yet,' said Mary. She saw my crestfallen face. 'But never mind,' she consoled, 'he does have a long way to come.'

'But I 'specially put some hay and oats in the barn for his reindeer,' I told her.

'I know,' said Pops, 'you go to the barn and feed the horses then come back for breakfast.'

Donning parka and woolly hat I headed along the path we'd dug out of the snow. Inside the barn, I found the empty stall had been trampled in, the hay very definitely nibbled and sticking out of the oat-box was a small, brown paper package. Poor old Belle and Captain were forgotten as I raced back to the house with my precious parcel. 'He's been, he's been,' I shouted as I burst through the door. 'And the reindeers have eaten the hay.'

The parcel was opened. It was a three-inch square book of Little Orphan Annie and by flicking through the pages, the tiny drawing in the top corner of each page appeared to move. It became one of my most treasured possessions.

We then exchanged gifts. I had drawn pictures for everyone. A cow for Pops, Buster the dog for Auntie Mum and a giant sunflower for Mary. In return I received a hankie, delicately crocheted around the edge, it was pretty enough for a Princess. Mary got one as well but hers only had daisies on it. Auntie Mum had knitted me a brown hood with flaps to stop my ears from freezing. She got a new bookmark for her bible, covered in pressed violets. But best of all, Pops announced he would build me a small cart and the first white calf born in the spring would be trained to pull it. He was very clever at making things. He'd built our house and this Christmas he'd carved a small bird for Mary and marquetry picture of deer nibbling grass in the moonlight for Auntie Mum.

After breakfast I went to help with the chores. After mucking out and feeding the stock we headed for the chicken coops. Pops drew my attention to something sticking out of a snowdrift behind the house. We went to investigate. There pointing to the leaden skies was a pair of ski's.

'What are they doing there?' I asked.

'Kris Kringle must have forgotten to leave them in the barn, so as he was passing over the house, he must have popped them over the side of his sleigh," he explained.

My first Christmas as an evacuee. Absolute magic.

First winter

In the corn

With Mary

Picture for home
with Pops and Auntie Mum

SPRING 1941

I was out and about as usual when I found a two pair of antlers, which were triumphantly carried home in my cart. I had no idea why they were on the ground. Mary explained that most horned animals keep their horns for life, but deer have new ones every year and it's in the spring that they fall off. "A bit like your milk teeth really, then they start growing new ones. But they start off all soft and furry."

That started me on my collection of horns. I would hunt high and low every spring to add to my collection. One day we were on our way to town, when I spotted some on the edge of a slough. I shouted excitedly to Pops, who reined in Belle and before we'd come to a stop, I'd leapt off and scrambled to collect the antlers. I tossed them in the back and we carried on, but this wasn't my only surprise that day.

As usual we popped into the general store, which doubled as a post office. Sometimes there would be mail from England or a package from Eaton's catalogue. This time I had two surprises. First I was introduced to an elderly, stooping man with a genial, flushed face and great, bushy side-whiskers. He was leaning against the counter.

"This is Peggy."

He solemnly held out his hand. He only had two fingers. "Heard all about you, young 'un. Enjoying it here?"

I nodded, I was concerned about his fingers.

"Learned to ride yet?"

I shook my head. "Not really."

"Ah well plenty of time for that, but don't you go falling off too often." He gave me a river of a smile. "All right little 'un, don't do nuthin silly now." And with a quick ruffle of my hair, he turned and walked out of the shop. I then realised his left leg was just a spike.

Pops explained he'd been a casualty of the prairies. Years earlier, he'd been out trapping and frozen his fingers and feet so badly that they'd had to amputate fingers on both hands, all the toes on his right leg, but his left leg had to be amputated above the knee. His wooden leg had a metal spike inserted at the bottom. He said he could walk better with it in. Pops said he used to go to the local dances and could whirl around with the best of them, but they made him take his spike out first.

When he'd finished the story, we were told there was a packet waiting for us. It wasn't from England though. I received those most months, dutifully read them, then under pressure from my new family, reply. My initial letters started Dear Mum and Dad, but eventually this changed to Dear Mother and Father. Anyway today was different. There was a packet for me! I started to unwrap it, but Pops retrieved it, telling me I had to wait 'till I got home.

Leaping down from the buckboard. I rushed to show Mary. She smiled. "We'd better open it then."

My fumbling fingers tore at the brown paper wrapping. Inside was my introduction to 'Post School.'

It was a preparatory course, before real school, for which the starting age in the prairies was eight. The lessons were basic and mostly of a religious nature. Mary and Auntie Mum were stern taskmasters and I was never allowed to skip a lesson. When completed, they were packaged and returned. Marked papers would be returned with the next lesson.

SUMMER 1941

The seasons were all explicit and extreme, dominating all our actions and our lives.

Summer saw the temperatures rise to over a hundred degrees. You could see animals staggering in the blazing sun as the heat lay over the prairies like an oppressive blanket. Cloudless skies glared down on us, but the intense heat of summer usually brought spectacular storms and when the first growls of thunder were heard, we knew we'd have a ringside seat in a theatre of spectacle.

Hail storms were the worst. Stones, the size of large marbles would smash down the ripening corn in minutes. In the house, we would grab every available blanket or cushion, padding them up against the windows in an effort to protect them from those deadly missiles.

At first I was blissfully unaware of the havoc they were wreaking, because after the very first one I'd witnessed, Auntie Mum sent me to collect a pail full of 'stones.' She then crushed them and using salt as a sort of freezing agent and putting one pail inside another, she conjured up ice-cream.

Lightening could be witnessed in all its glory, I was always amazed at its ferocity. But nature compensated as it scattered in a multitude of dazzling forks or exploded in a luminous sheet across the whole leaden sky. Storms went as quickly as they arrived. The transformation scene was breathtaking.

First, the air came alive with an assortment of winged creatures. Sheltering birds now swooped and skimmed in the cool, fresh air, tossing rainbows as they flew. Butterflies appeared like sugared wafers in the breeze, while humming birds hovered in a diamond haze, vying for nectar with the bumblebees, who infused the air like giant cake crumbs.

The lake became a myriad of movement. It was like looking at a splash of deep blue paint spilled out onto an artist's canvas. Innumerable insects skating and leaping. Moorhens plopping and chicks scooting across the surface.

The intermittent crash of distant thunder could still be heard. Three seconds, three miles away, four seconds, four miles away, now it was becoming someone else's problem.

As the dark, threatening skies scurried away, I could see iceberg clouds bearing down on fairy tale castles which drifted into the distant horizon.

Soon we were back to normal. But what was normal? My life was certainly not normal, but yet it was not abnormal.

It certainly wasn't ordinary. But was it extraordinary?

Yes, I decided it was extraordinary. I didn't even get 'ordinary' illnesses.

I'd never had a cold, but I did have a cow that stood on my foot and a colt that catapulted me through the air like a bullet. Oh, and a crazy chicken once took a lump out of my leg and an even crazier turkey chased me up a tree, but I got away with grazed knees and cramp from hanging on until he strutted back to the barn. Marauding mink, you already know about. In fact the only one that gave the family cause for concern was the time a rusty nail embedded itself in my hand.

I had enthusiastically been trying to demonstrate my skills at roping on an unsuspecting heifer. She viewed the whole episode with great suspicion and became increasingly unpredictable. Deciding enough was enough, she glared, snorted a few times, then charged. I stopped dead in my tracks, not prepared for this turn of events. Nostrils flaring and tail threshing about like a convulsive snake, she headed directly at me. I leapt over the corral fence but in my frantic attempts to jump clear caught my hand on a nail.

It was very painful and deeply inflamed for several days, but with the ever-trusty salt water and iodine it soon cleared up, but left me with a jagged reminder for many years.

Every summer Mary would take me on a picnic. Packing a wicker basket with newly baked bread and chunks of ham and cheese we would head for a pasture. As meticulous as ever she would spread small, blue gingham tablecloth on the meadow grass, so all was proper and correct.

Sitting there in our luxuriant Kingdom, we would try to capture the sights and sounds surrounding us.

Watching us, watching them, were a selection of curious animals, none more so than the ubiquitous Gopher.

The 'Prairie Dog,' is everywhere, especially near wheat.

It's a greyish, brown rodent, about ten inches long, with a light coloured pencil tail. It burrows deep into the ground, but spends most of its time running about the surface, eating grain in all its stages of development.

The gopher is dull witted and has a stupid habit of sitting on the edge of it hole, chirping and jerking its tail before scuttling to safety underground. It's a favourite meal of hawks, weasels and coyotes.

With a gestation period of only one-month, it raises an immense family of up to two dozen at a time!

The gopher's burrow is a masterpiece of engineering. It has several rooms, including a hibernating chamber and a nursery, constructed so heavy rains cannot destroy it.

Although the gopher is a great pest, it does play an important part in the uncultivated grassland. By their digging, it stirs up and aerates the soil. But you'd better watch out if you're out riding because of a horse catches its foot in the burrow, it can easily break a leg and the rider will be catapulted out of the saddle.

I'd been telling Pops about how many of theses animals we'd seen in the meadow and he asked me if I'd like to go out and help him set some poison for the gopher population.

We set out with two pails full of poisoned wheat. He said this had been done ever since the settlers first planted on the prairies. Every time we found a hole, we would spoon some of the mixture into the burrow entrance. It worked reasonably well. A predator, usually a crow often devoured the few that expired above ground, so we managed to get rid of two pests for the price of one!

A few weeks later I was aware that the house seemed to be a hive of industry.

"We're getting ready for sports day," said Mary.

"What, here at the farm?"

"No, silly, it's at Ravine School. It happens every year and everybody goes."

I found out that the school was used for picnics, dances, masquerades, box socials, whist drives and of course the annual summer fete. I was told that was highly regarded day out for all the family.

Pops, Auntie Mum and Mary all put baskets filled with goodies, which were going to be sold, in the back of the buggy.

When we arrived it was already heaving with every imaginable sort crafts. Lace work, knitting, crochet, embroidery and masterpieces of carved woodwork. Pops soon added his marquetery pictures. And you wouldn't believe the selection of cakes, cookies and preserves.

But the biggest surprise of all was a merry-go-round, built by George Antonishen and Walter Sotski. It could hold eight people, all in individual chairs. Ropes attached them to a long pole, which in turn was connected to a heavy central pole. It was a huge success, with adults as well as children trying it out.

Popular though it was, easily the favourite was the home-made candy stall. Mary's contribution was Candied Rose petals.

They were real pretty and tasted like proper candy. The following summer I found out how she made them.

First paint some rose water on each side of a petal then sprinkle it with very fine castor sugar and leave in the sun to 'candy'. Turn the petals frequently, occasionally sprinkling them with rose water and sugar 'till they became crisp. Never tried it in England though.

Another recipe she taught me was for rose petal jelly.

First you get some apples or gooseberries, slice the fruit, without peeling. Cover with water and simmer until it's a pulp. Strain through a bag and allow one pint to every pound of preserving sugar. Warm and stir until the sugar is dissolved and then put in as many rose petals as the liquor will hold. Boil until the jelly sets. Test it on a cold plate. When ready, strain and put in hot jars. I was told on good authority that's how the settlers did it.

AUTUMN 1941

Dennis was home on leave and Auntie Mum wanted to make him some of his favourite hazelnut cookies, so I was sent out to collect a pound or so of nuts. There was a wood about three hundred yards from the house which was an absolute haven for them. As I was discarding the husks I thought I heard Pops and Dennis talking so went to investigate. I soon found them in a small clearing. Dennis was aiming a rifle at a white horse, tethered to a tree in front of him. I head a loud crack and watched as the beast crumbled to the floor. It lay very still. Pops and Dennis went over to the animal and they started to cut up the carcass. I decided to come out of hiding and see what they were doing. Dennis looked up as I approached. He grinned and holding the entrails aloft shouted: "Hey look at these. We can now have sausages for tea."

After inspecting them I told them I was going to tell Mary and Auntie Mum.

Rushing through the door I excitedly shouted, "We're having sausages for tea. Dennis said so. He's bringing them from the horse now."

Auntie Mum took a deep breath and glared at me. "Upstairs to bed this instant."

I had already learned not to argue, so turned immediately on my heel and puzzled, made my way upstairs.

I was peering out of my window, wondering what I'd done wrong, when all hell seemed to break loose downstairs.

I could clearly hear Auntie Mum. "Why on earth did you allow a child to watch you?" she screamed. I'd never heard her so angry.

First she was incensed I'd witnessed the shooting, albeit unintentionally, but she was incandescent that the stripping of the carcass had not been withheld from my gaze. The 'sausage' joke was the last straw. It all went quiet so decided it would be safe for me to go back downstairs. The minute I entered the room, Mary snapped. "Were you told to come back down?" I shook my head. She turned to her mother. "Is it all right?"

Auntie Mum just gave a curt nod and continued with her baking. I headed for the outside door. "But you stay indoors."

With that tone of voice I had no intention of going anywhere.

When Pops and Dennis came in for their meal, Dennis sat opposite me and gave me a great big wink. It was our secret. I felt my shoulders hunch up with pleasure, but I daren't smile too much. Dennis had a wide engaging smile that tipped to one side and made you feel special. I felt better already.

The next day and it was all back to normal.

The same year I heard my first pig slaughter. It was an event, normally executed – if you'll excuse the pun – in the autumn, but after the horse fiasco, to make sure I was out of the way, I'd been sent to check on the cattle in the far pasture. But as usual I'd run there and after a quick chase around the field with a few bullocks I raced back. As I neared the house I heard the most agonising screams. I came around the corner of the pigsty and found myself in the midst of the annual slaughter. The animal was hanging by it's back legs, having just had its throat cut and was being slowly immersed in a large drum of boiling water, kept hot by a roaring brush fire underneath.

Horror struck I sped from the grizzly scene, the horrendous screams ringing in my ears.

I went to locate Snowflake, my little white calf, hitched him to my cart and travelled for as far as possible, trying to erase the sound of that tortuous death.

That cart was my transport of delight. It ferried anything from baby chicks to cabbages, strawberries to dead gophers – not at the same time, I hasten to add - I did try to ferry the cats in it, but they objected - strongly.

Pigs were not my favourite animals. These fat, ugly, smelly animals seemed to spend their days constantly snuffling and guzzling, so other than help feed them a revolting grey slop, consisting mainly of general household mush, I stayed clear. Anyway I was terrified of the cantankerous old boar, although I quite enjoyed the antics of the babies, but thought nothing of it when it was time to take them into town in varying stages of growth to sell.

Occasionally we would take an adult, but we usually kept them for breeding and when they became unable to produce more litters, they became our winter meat supply.

It was idyllic. Cities, noise and family were completely forgotten. I had not played with another child for over a year, but I never missed the companionship.

I loved going to town with Pops. It was always just the two of us. Neither Auntie Mum nor Mary ever accompanied us, in fact you seldom saw any wives in the stores.

When we passed other farmers on the trail, Pops would nod his head in acknowledgement. Were these 'nodding; acquaintances I ask myself.

Some pulled up their rigs for the inevitable discussion on the state of the crops. One day Mr Schukart, pulled up his old grey mare to have a short chat. He was a familiar sight with his wide-brimmed, black felt hat, pulled into a comfortable shape around his head. Like other farmers he was nearly always on his own.

"Howya doin'?"

"Lost some turkeys in that storm."

Pops shook his head knowingly. "How's Maisie. Back any better?"

"Oh, my God," said Mr Schukart. "I've left her in the bloody town."

With that he'd turned his rig round and galloped back towards Leross.

Cutting the grain, ready to harvest was now a priority and I was soon found a job.

The binder tossed the sheaves well clear of the stubble, so the horses wouldn't trample it on their return journey.

It was my job to collect the untied, ejected corn and put it into bunches for Mary to hand tie. All the sheaves were then piled into stooks to dry out, ready for the threshing machine.

Even at seven years of age I was expected to help in the back aching job of stooking. Picking up the sheaves you would lean the tops together, forming a tunnel to allow the air through. Usually three sheaves each side. I got a few nasty thorns and cuts when I grabbed hold of a sheaf bristling with thistles. Nobody warned me but I soon learnt to look out for them.

After a couple of weeks, I was instructed to fill the small shed, in which we stretched pelts, with fresh hay.

The kitchen was a hive of activity, Auntie Mum and Mary were baking mounds of bread and pasties. More instructions. "Go into the garden and bring back, thirty heads of corn, four pumpkins, six turnips and ten beetroot." A perfect job for my little cart.

The following morning all was revealed. The farmers were in a co-operative, formed in 1924 and they shared a communal thresher. They would harvest crops one by one, moving around the area until all the grain was safely stored.

As the gang moved across to the first field, I was told to bring one of the barrels from the back of the barn and place it on the south side of the house.

Task completed I ran inside. "Now fill it with water from the well," ordered Mary.

You could only get one pail at a time, so it meant trolling backwards and forwards until there was anything like enough. It was about a hundred yards to the well and I started off at a trot, slowing considerably until I was all spent out. Pulling the pail up became more and more exhausting, I guess I must have lugged about seventeen pails to and from the barrel.

"Finished," I said proudly as I slumped onto the bench seat.

"Not yet you haven't," said Mary. "You now have to take that little table near the stove and put it next to the barrel."

I wearily got up and picked up the table, but I hadn't even got through the door when she barked, "And put that old tin jug and basin on it."

I had had no idea why, but obeyed without question.

When all the men came in after the day's toil, they needed to wash down. That's where my barrel came in. As it had been in the sun all day the water was now quite warm. Nearby were some towels for them to dry off.

Their shirts were shaken out but put back on, as Auntie Mum wouldn't allow bare torsos to be displayed in the house. After supper, shirts would be laid over some bushes to air out. They slept in their vest and pants.

As soon as the wheat was threshed, it would be hauled to the elevators in Leross, where an agent would grade it. The appearance and plumpness of the kernel and its weight determined the price.

When it had been loaded onto the train it would be shipped to all corners of the globe. Pops said that the very first shipment of Prairie grain went to Great Britain in 1876 and some was taken to Hull and Rank's flourmill, where they had played as children. It's a funny Old World.

Binder waiting to go

Dennis and Pops threshing

Collecting the sheaves

WINTER 1941/2

I soon got used to the solitude. Evenings were quiet and ordered affairs but every night saw the same ritual. First we sat quietly, letting our meal settle – Auntie Mum's idea – Pops would enjoy a cigarette, but was soon in the kitchen working with his tiny marquetry saw, cutting through the delicate wood with precision. He created works of art which he sold at the annual fair and school sports day. Sometimes he allowed me to have a go. A square moon had a fetching quality about it!

Pops also showed me how to make doll's furniture from cast off cotton reels, some cardboard and small scraps of discarded material. Even though I didn't have a doll's house, it kept me amused and quiet!

Mary and I often sat shelling peas, but Mary preferred painting in water-colours and pressing flowers. Knitting, sewing and crochet were Auntie Mum's recreational pastimes. After about an hour she would put her work in a saggy woollen bag and go to pick up the huge family bible from the top of the stubby chest of drawers. You always knew it was time to put your work down as she invariably gave a deep heavy sigh before she rose.

She selected a reading, chosen earlier and we sat and inwardly digested the words of wisdom. When she closed the book, that was my signal to go to bed.

Once a week we all gathered around the radio and listened to Edgar Bergen and Charlie McCarthy, a ventriloquist and his dummy. Everyone was united in laughter. Batteries had a very short life so we had to ration our listening time, but we did occasionally tune in to a news programme.

I helped Pops build an ice-house. First he dug a deep hole and built a small shed over the top. Cutting lumps of ice from a nearby slough he dropped them in the hole, then poured water over them and let it freeze solid. The whole lot was liberally covered with sawdust to prevent melting at a later date. Hey presto, a home-made refrigerator, keeping things like butter, cream and meat edible during the summer months.

SPRING 1942

I was now eight years old and given more exacting and strenuous tasks around the farm. Manure spreading was one of them. I would load up a raft contraption, called a stoneboat - it was made up of 2" by 6" planks, about six feet long, fastened to two thick, polar runners and pulled by a horse – from the pile which had accumulated outside the barns. It was steaming and very pungent! It weighed down the raft so much only Captain, our strongest horse could pull it. Once he got going his gentle plod was just about right, then with a fork I sprayed the foul smelling nutrients onto the land.

I was piling the last load of manure onto the 'boat' when Pops came across.

"Last lot for you. Next week you start school."

Nobody had said a word.

"What on my own?"

"Nope. Mary'll take you."

"Can I go on horseback?"

"No," said Pops, "It's not that far. You'll be walking."

It was two miles away.

The school had been there for over thirty years. It was built in 1911 after the settlers realised if their children were to get an education, they'd have to organise the building of a school.

The Minister of Education immediately gave permission, so they set to and built a school. Nearly everyone in the community helped in some way or other, but my uncles, Allan and Herman Collingwood did most of the difficult woodwork.

It was named after the ravine that ran along the back of the land.

The initial enrolment accounted for thirteen children, the number insisted upon by the Government for a new school. The parents had to take turns at being 'teacher', although that proved quite tricky in the early 1900's as not many of the settlers spoke English, but several families were Swedish, so they managed. It took two years before a suitable tutor could be found.

There was not a 'true' Canadian amongst the students. The nationalities included German, Czechoslavakian, Ukrainian, Scandinavian, Poles, Chinese and British, yet they all sang O'Canada with great pride and passion.

Our pile of hay was diminishing fast and I was invited to be part of the circus that exposed the last layer. The hay, which had been carefully stacked in the fall, was systematically used from the top, layer by layer. I often took great forkfuls into the barn, so wondered why Dad had asked me to be there.

"Why is it special?" I asked.

"Well, you know that once the stack is built it becomes the home for multitudes of rats and mice don't you?"

I shrugged my shoulders. I hadn't really thought about it. Pops gave that slow gentle smile and sort of cocked his head to one side. I swear I saw him wink!

There was now only a thin layer of fodder left but just before we started to fork it away, Pops whistled and as if my magic, Buster and innumerable cats appeared from nowhere. They circled in anticipation. They obviously knew something I didn't.

"Now!" shouted Pops, "Start digging."

With swift upward motions, the forks tossed away the final covering, exposing the unsuspecting rodents.

Buster and the cats knew Christmas had come early. The ground was alive with scurrying animals, the mice scrambling in a feverish haste to disperse to safer territory. The cats pounced, the dog chased but any that looked like showing a clean pair of heels were unceremoniously forked. I soon joined in and would hold my fork up in triumph with skewered mice squeaking in terror and pain.

Life and death were accepted with equanimity in this environment. It was only a matter of time before Pops said: "Come on, about time you killed a chicken for yourself."

We headed for the hencoops. Grabbing an unsuspecting hen he grabbed it by the legs and with a swift flick, turned it so it's head lay across a bloody block of wood. He brought down the axe blade in one vicious blow. I watched in fascination as it carried out its last macabre dance. I was then shown how to clean and pluck poultry.

The following day it was my turn. Without any compunction or compassion I be-headed a squirming, squawking hen.

Today I'm virtually a vegetarian and without doubt, if I were faced with the same scenario, that chicken would have nothing to worry about. Vegetables become more attractive by the minute. It makes me feel queasy just writing about it.

Throughout the summer months all kids went barefoot and we were all impatient for the snows to melt and gain our freedom again.

Every time I ventured outside the rebuke was the same. "Don't you dare take off your sneakers. It's too dangerous until the snow has melted and you can see what you're treading on."

Did I take any notice? Not a chance.

I'd gone out as usual and safe from prying eyes removed my sneakers. Hanging them around my neck I jauntily ventured to the lake to watch the explosion of nature.

As I was leaping and bounding around, my foot slipped against a jagged rock, hidden by snow. It was bleeding quite heavily so I pressed it against the icy cold and watched as rivulets of red made patterns in the virgin white. It soon stopped, so my sneakers were hastily put back on.

My journey home was not quite as rapid or joyful.

Casually I walked through the door, washed my hands ready for supper and sat at the table. My foot was throbbing and sore, but I daren't limp.

After the meal a bowl was brought for me to get a strip wash.

"Come on take your sneakers off."

"No, it's all right, I'll take them off upstairs."

"You'll do no such thing. Get them off NOW!"

I sat dumbly on the small stool. Unsuccessfully Mary tried to relieve me of my sandshoe. The blood had stuck it very firmly to my foot.

I had to own up.

My foot, with shoe still attached, was immersed in a bowl of warm water until it could be eased away.

It was washed with salt water, then the farmer's friend, the ever-trusty iodine, was poured over the wound.

When it had been bandaged, Pops stepped forward, up to then neither he nor Auntie Mum had uttered a word.

"You were told about taking your shoes off and you purposefully disobeyed."

The Pops with the normally placid disposition was now showing another layer. One I didn't like.

He took his leather-shaving strop from its hook on the back door.

"Take down your pants."

I obeyed immediately.

Leaning over the three-legged milking stool, I received two stinging slaps from the leather strop.

I did not flinch or utter a sound – I got up – adjusted my

overalls and slowly walked past Mary and Auntie Mum, who were now busy sewing and did not even glance my way.

The following morning the smarting weals could be seen distinctly.

Downstairs everything was normal. The incident was never mentioned again. They assumed the lesson had been learned. It had!

Only two days later Pops asked: "Want to see some Grouse dancing?"

I thought he was teasing, but as I'd found out a long time ago, Pops did not tease. I jumped at the chance although I hadn't a clue what I was about to see.

We had to set off early in the morning as they only perform as the sun is rising.

Evidently, the Sharp Tailed Grouse is normally very wary, but their instinct to dance drive these birds to such a state of frenzy that they lose all fear of man. As we reached a small clearing in 'Owl's Bluff,' they were already in full dance mode on a mound of earth. We quietly sneaked behind some thick bushes. We watched as they cavorted with heads down, neck arched and wings spread fan-tailed to the ground. Each tail was a stiff as a ramrod and the back of it just a mass of fluffy white feathers.

"See that yellow on the top of his head?" Pops whispered. I nodded.

"Can't usually see that," he said, "Only when they fluff their feathers up to do the dance."

I was getting cramp in the same position and as I tried to move I tumbled onto the bush. Within seconds the birds had shot off in all directions. I was disappointed but I'd seen enough to entrance me for years.

My first day at school.

Mary walked with me to Ravine School. She had insisted I wore a dress. I hated it. All my days were spent in dungarees. I thought the days of wearing dresses were well gone. But Auntie Mum and Mary would have none of it.

The schoolhouse was a one room stuccoed affair, built at the end of a field, with two biffys, one for boys and one for girls. When everyone had finished with their Eaton's catalogue, they would bring it to school to use in the biffys. In front of the porch proudly stood the obligatory flagpole.

There were a lot of children running around but I was taken inside to meet the teacher Merle B. Vaughn. A slim, neat individual, with a mop of corn-coloured hair, which dropped in tendrils around a smiling, face. When she laughed, wrinkles spread out alarmingly in all directions.

Teachers taught all subjects to all grades. Mary handed me my lunch box, a can of water and bundle of books.

"You can come part of the way back home with the Srochinski's and Choats, then take the trail to the farm," she said, gave me a half-smile, then turned and marched briskly out of the door.

The room was high and square, lines of desks were arranged neatly in rows. It was dominated by a huge wood burning stove which stood near the blackboard.

Miss Vaughn was pointing at a desk. "This will be yours. Do you want to put your things inside?"

I did.

"Follow me," Said Miss Vaughn.

I followed.

She stood on the porch and rung a hand bell and all the children ran and formed a circle around the flagpole. A fair-haired girl with bobbing curls smiled and held out her hand, I joined the circle. Miss Vaughn slowly raised the Canadian flag, while everyone sang the National Anthem, O' Canada.

I found out during the ensuing years, that ritual was carried out regardless of how inclement the weather might be.

Everyone then filed in and sat at their desk, determined by age. For the whole of my years in the prairies, I can proudly boast I came top of my class every term. But don't tell anyone I was the only one in it will you?

The government supplied readers, but we had to supply pens and paper. At noon huge pots of cocoa were made for us.

When the temperature dropped to five or ten below, we would huddle around the stove to get warm, the heat only spread for about six feet, so most of us sat in our coats. When it was really cold, our bread and cheese would have frozen solid. Can't ever remember bothering about it.

Several children went to school on horseback – Some riding two to a horse and others travelled in a buggy or democrat.

The barn was big enough to hold seven or eight horses, but in fine weather the animals were tethered to a long pole attached to the side. All had an oat bag attached their halter.

At recess I was soon introduced to the boisterous game 'Prisoners Base,' as the ages ranged from eight to sixteen, games were usually something which all could join in. The whole school (which amounted to twenty to twenty-four pupils) divided into two teams. Parallel lines were already marked with stones at each end of the field. The object was to invade the opposite territory without being 'tagged.'

Baseball was also played, but on my first day it caused me a bloody nose. I had been dismissed to the outfield with the other younger children. The ball came hurtling towards me, but I couldn't catch it and it hit the ground, bounced up and struck me squarely on the nose. The teacher rushed me to the water barrel and ducked my head in the water, then ordered me to the schoolroom for the rest of the period. I think that hurt more than the bloodied nose.

When I set off home I was accompanied by Mike and Joe Schochinski, George Horvath and Joyce Erikson. The Choats had already disappeared in a cloud of dust.

I was the only one heading east. When we came to the fork in the road, we exchanged muted farewells, but as time progressed we would set out with much shouting and waving until we were out of sight and sound of each other. We usually yodelled as we found that particular method of keeping in touch transmitted further than any other sound we could make.

As I got older and learnt to ride, recess became an exciting time. I would join some of my compatriots in riding Indian style. No saddles or bridles. We would gallop at full pelt and try to pick up objects from the ground – without falling off! Many a time a child could be seen swinging from the mane of a horse travelling at speed while they tried to pick something off the ground, cheered on by the whole school, especially when they fell off.

Sometimes we'd have a go at standing on the back of a horse and with the rashness of youth, see how far we could get without tumbling to earth. The older pupils would stand astride two horses and try to make the end of the field, but even at a gentle trot the horses could not be properly reined in and they soon parted company, with each other as well as the rider. That got the biggest cheer of all. We would have made a pretty nifty circus act.

Although we were frequently bruised and grazed no one got seriously injured.

Once summer was upon us we started practising for sports day. Parents were industrious for weeks, knitting, crocheting, making cakes, jams, pickles, the list was endless. They were sold at a stall on the day. It was especially constructed out of logs and an awning of branches, on the north of the building, to keep everything cool while the goodies on display were surveyed.

You would see hand-made dollies, embroidered table-cloths, pressed flowers, home-made wines, wood carvings and best of all Mrs Phillips ice-cream.

The selection of eatables would grace any restaurant.

On the field everybody entered everything. Usually divided

as near as possible to age groups. At the end of the day, winners battled against each other, so we had an overall champion.

The high jump was my special. I was champion every year, beating boys and girls. Pops built me my very own 'jump.' Nails at varying heights were a support for the peeled aspen branch, which was laid across the upright posts. Bruises on my legs proved how difficult it was to knock off as it got caught on the nail head. Hour after hour I practised. Mary took a picture of Dennis and me beside the jump and it won a 'Happy evacuee' prize in a newspaper.

I loved running, but only long distances. I was hopeless at the hundred-yard dash. I could never master the explosive start. A mediocre fizzle was about my lot. The longest race was ten times around the school perimeter. Usually I was the only girl taking part and I did win – once!

At school I cannot recall anyone ever being chastised. Miss Lillico, who took over from Miss Vaughn, was strict but fair. We all liked and respected her. Also of course, we would have had our parent's wrath to contend with if we hadn't got our heads down and shown good results from our labours.

Betty Lillico had the most infectious giggle, if something amused her she found it hard to control herself and in no time at all the whole room would be joining in. She would shuffle to the back of the class, bring herself under control, then walk sedately to the front and order us to continue with our lessons.

Ravine School

School room

First day of school

On school steps

Sports day

l/r front row, Joe Shrochinski,
George Horvath,
Mike Shrochinski
Back, Anne Katelnakoff, Betty
Lillico (teacher), Joyce Ericson

SUMMER 1942

One day while racing along with a couple of heifers I noticed two horses in the distance rearing and striking out at each other, their necks arched in fury as they attempted to sink their bared teeth into each others flesh. They were scrapping across a barbed wire fence, making it even more dangerous. I suddenly realised one of the horses was my lovely gentle Belle. I watched in horror as with hoofs flailing the air, she crashed forward into the post holding the wire and it plunged deep into her chest. A state of panic momentarily overcame me. I watched in horror a she lay writhing and screaming in agony. All the other beasts in the pasture were stampeding in terror.

Blood was pouring from the wound. I had to find Pops. My feet hardly touched the ground as I raced back to the house. He was mending a fence near the big corral. I screamed and waved to attract his attention. Speed was of the essence, I knew that.

"Harness Captain to the stoneboat and take it to the pasture," he shouted while running to the house to collect Mary and give Auntie Mum instructions on what to prepare.

Poor old Captain didn't know what had hit him when I kept slapping his backside to hustle him into the harness. The sledge kept slipping and sliding on the uneven ground, but I was riding Captain and could urge him forward. Back in the pasture Pops and Mary had already roped Belle down and removed the stake and blood was pouring out of a gaping wound while her breath was coming in short, painful gasps. They were desperately trying to calm her.

As Mary held her whiskered muzzle in both hands, she turned her head and her deep brown eyes were filled with pleading for us to help her. It was pitiful. Pops plugged the wound as best he could with his shirt, to try and stem the bleeding, but blood was already seeping through.

Ropes were attached to the harness and I slowly led captain forward, while Mary and Pops tried to pull the old mare as gently as possible onto the Stoneboat. They pushed and heaved to a point of exhaustion, while the struggling mare objected. She was getting weaker by the minute. Belle was losing copious amounts of blood and I think Pops was sure we'd lose her, but she they eventually managed to load her onto the 'boat.'

Belle was a big, fat old thing and we thought the initial strain of starting to pull her weight was going to be too much, even for Captain. It was a slow and tortuous journey back to the barn where Auntie Mum was waiting. She helped haul Belle inside. I was sharply told to "Stay outside."

Sitting on a nearby corral fence, sneakers drumming impatiently on the lowest bar, I desperately wanted to help.

The ripped and torn flesh was cleaned up and salt water was poured over the gaping wound, it was then liberally covered with a tar like substance. Poor Belle was in agony and her shrill screams burst around the barn. Swallows dipped and swooped around their heads in their haste to get outside and all the animals in the vicinity stampeded to escape from the tortured, penetrating shrieks.

I heard those screams for years.

After what seemed an eternity, all was quiet in the barn. I was now allowed in. Belle lay motionless in the straw. They let her rest for a while and then tried to get her to stand, as it was dangerous for a horse to lie for long periods.

It took days of careful nursing and sleepless nights for Pops and Mary who took it in turns to sleep in the barn. They knew they'd turned the corner when she tried her first few faltering steps.

No victory could have been sweeter. I was now given the easy bit. Tempting her to eat properly and walk a little further each day, building her confidence as well as her stamina.

All I used was a halter when I took her on our morale boosting walks. We had made our leisurely way to a field to pick some Sennaca root. This was widely used in the prairies as an old Indian medication for rheumatism and I could earn myself a few cents by collecting the root and selling it in town.

Belle was quietly grazing nearby as I busily dug away in a small patch. I became aware of a figure standing behind me. I looked around.

A striking, weather-beaten face, with piercing black eyes, glowered down at me, arms folded menacingly. His long, jet-black hair was held in place by a brightly beaded headband across his forehead.

I was meeting my first Indian. In his moccasins I noticed a small knife slipped into the top. I didn't wait to see anything else. Belle instantly set off when this demented child suddenly leapt upon her back, with arms and legs flailing in terror I urged her forward at full speed.

Now Belle was a tall horse, about fifteen hands, and decidedly fat, normally I couldn't mount her unless I was standing on a stone or with assistance. This day I made it in one. She did me proud and set off at a brisk trot. Well quite brisk anyway! I'd forgotten all about her injury.

I daren't look round "Don't go near the Indians." "Stay away from the Indian camps." The warnings were ringing in my ears.

The farmers had scant time for them. They roamed the land with their wagons and a contraption called a 'travois', which consisted of two poles, dragged behind a horse, with some of their belongings lashed to it. Spare horses, in a variety of colours, with matted manes and tails, would be tied behind the wagons. Indians never used saddles, just richly coloured blankets tossed over the horses back. They would cut through any fence barring their way, leaving a trail of destruction in their wake. That meant horses and cattle could wander at will and as nearly all the fences were constructed with barbed wire, many were injured on the trailing barbs.

The tribe, usually a party of ten to fifteen, would choose a site and set up camp. Tee-pees were erected and fires lit. Three or four would then be despatched into town to bargain for food, after staying for three or four days the itinerants would be on their way, led by a lone Indian on horseback.

The Sennaca root, along with blankets and beaded apparel were swapped for provisions. The Indian I encountered probably thought I was poaching on his patch, whatever the reason for his sudden appearance, I didn't wait to find out if it was friendship he was after!

I urged Belle to go faster. Pops had seen us from across the pasture and ran towards us shouting. I've never seen him so angry in my life. Come to think of it, I'd never seen him really angry. I pulled up Belle and gulping in large mouthfuls of air, gabbled out.

"There was an Indian and he was going to get me. He had a knife and everything." Pops helped me down and I was asked to explain. He listened carefully, with just a few well chosen 'mmm's,' a shake of the head and an almost startled 'dearie, dearie me.' Belle's wound was closely inspected, "Mmm," he muttered. "No harm done." Then turned on his heel and went back to his ploughing.

Only a few days after my encounter with the Blackfoot, I was herding the cattle back to the barn, when suddenly the air was cut with the whinney of a horse. I saw an unfamiliar flash of scarlet riding across the pastures. As it cantered towards me I realised we had a real-life Mountie visiting us. I ran to greet him in great excitement. He rode with a carbine (a short barrelled rifle) slung from his saddle and a revolver at his hip.

Stationed in posts throughout Canada, a sort of combined military and police force, they policed hundreds of thousands of square miles in all weathers and they managed to keep order in those isolated regions.

Having received many reports of marauding Indians, smashing their way through the fields and pastures in our area, they had decided to investigate.

He'd just ridden over from Kelliher, where an old Indian had been reported for firing a rifle at passing trains, then as he galloped through town, he would take pot-shots at the Protestant and Catholic churches. He didn't show up while the Mountie was there, but he told us later: "As he didn't kill anybody, there wasn't much I could do about it and anyway he really wasn't doing much harm."

He was made welcome and I was given the job of feeding and watering his horse. I'd never seen such a sinewy animal. His coat gleamed like burnished copper. Bet he didn't pull many ploughs.

As soon as I'd tethered, watered and fed him, I raced back to the house and stood staring in awe at our unusual visitor, especially at the revolver.

He had been given refreshments and they were deep in conversation discussing the troublesome Indians.

Pops was explaining how it sometimes took days to locate straying animals. I listened intently. When it was obvious the serious talk was over I began my torrent of questions. Where? When? What? How?

He good-naturedly answered all my queries.

THE MOUNTIES REPLY

The North West Mounted Police were formed by the Government in 1867, initially to try and establish peaceful relations with the Indians, also to try and abolish their thriving liqueur trade.

They considered it an impossible mission but established a centre near the Farewell Trading Post. This became the site of the Cypress Hills massacre, where a group of whisky peddlers slaughtered a small band of peaceful Indians.

The population at that time consisted of several thousand white settlers and about three thousand Indians, mainly Assibone and Cree, with a large number of Metis. I go into detail about the Metis and other tribes in my book, 'Beyond The Brave', as Pops and his brother Herman were very involved with the Indians and lived with them for several years in the early 1900's.

Indians fascinated me. I knew nothing of their culture or behaviour. I had only heard of their marauding ways, which so enraged the local populace. So my questions were endless. I asked if we had Sioux Indians in Saskatchewan.

"A few," he answered, "They came over in the late 1800's and although they said they had only peaceful intentions, we took some persuading as they had a ferocious reputation."

He said Indians founded a Ghost Dance religion that was regularly performed and was ardently followed by all the tribes, "but it was probably the Sioux who introduced the sacred 'ghost shirt' worn by men and women."

Later in life I researched this shirt and evidently the basic design is the same for all tribes. Made from buckskin, muslin or cotton sewn together with sinew. Each garment was decorated with symbols, which were revealed to the dancer in a vision, during a trance like state.

However the Sioux believed it had the magical power to render the wearer invisible to the white man's bullets, with obvious results!

When they realised the shirt did not protect them, they changed to a dream inspired 'medicine bundle.' This was an array of religious talismen and herbs, which were used in a ceremony to ward off harm on the eve of a battle. It became the Sioux warrior's most precious possession.

Old Chief Sitting Bull's collection consisted of a wooden bowl with a stone pestle surrounded by herbs. A turtle shell cup and inside was, a wild radish, a rattle, some birch bark, an eagle's bone, a pouch of sacred paint and the skin of a mink stuffed with ten herbal remedies. The old chief had once made a speech, stating that all his people wanted was freedom and he'd never seen anything the white man had, that was as good as freedom and that included houses, trains and clothes.

My Mountie gave me a real insight into the Indians and a thirst for more information about the wilderness years in the prairies. As he galloped off, I ran after him waving enthusiastically until he turned right at 'Owls Bluff', stampeding a small herd of deer and I could see him no more.

Of all animals, the deer can best adapt to life on the prairies. Their food consists almost entirely of weeds and grass.

Fawns are born early in the spring and for the first few months lie perfectly still in the long grass. They never move except to feed from their mothers.

Once while picking wild strawberries, I was aware of large, brown expressive eyes looking right at me. It was a fawn, nestled down in long meadow grass. The urge to pet it was overwhelming, but I knew it should be left.

I looked for its mother but could see nothing. Moving away to some bushes about a hundred yards away, I crouched and waited. It must have been nearly an hour before I spotted the doe. She tentatively inched forward, her head held high, eyes darting, nostrils flaring. About a yard from her young, she snorted a greeting and it leapt from the long grass and delightedly nuzzled for milk. But this wasn't the time for feeding, mum wanted to rejoin the safety of the herd as quickly as possible, even a small fawn can outrun man, so it wasn't long before they were a speck on the horizon.

In July and August my golden sunflowers, which had been sown in an arc around the vegetable patch, stood tall and proud, stretching upwards to over ten feet tall, their heads bent over, heavy with ripening seeds. They are delicious, especially when baked in a seedcake. One day while concentrating on pulling over a thick stem, I failed to notice an unwelcome visitor. A skunk!

They are conspicuously marked, with a long bushy tail. When you see that tail go up, you run. Fast! In fact, at the speed of light. The scent of the anal glands can be shot over twelve feet. I didn't run fast enough. The aim was perfect. The smell indescribable. My clothes had to be burned.

The skunk is practically immune from attack from predators. I now knew why. But skunks aren't the only unwelcome visitor to the prairies, I found mosquitoes in abundance. The first summer I was bitten unreservedly as I slapped and swatted, but immunity soon set in. Everyone still got bitten and they were still a flaming nuisance, especially near the lake but the soreness and itching reduced considerably. When they were really bad we built smudges for the animals. That meant putting a huge mound of wet straw on a roaring fire. The subsequent smoke did help keep them at bay.

I'd been checking on the smudges and putting out some salt blocks for the animals when Pops shouted: "Going to town, are you coming?"

While he was harnessing captain, I was getting changed. Auntie Mum forbade me from travelling to town in my dungarees.

At the post office there was a letter from my mother to Pops and Auntie Mum. It told them she was going to talk to me via the radio.

I found out later that CORB had sent a circular inviting parents to use an opportunity given by the BBC to send messages to their children. It was headlined 'Broadcast Message.' And read; "If you have not already recorded a message to be broadcast to your child and would like to do so, you should write to Miss Maxwell, Broadcasting House, London W1. Mention your name and address, your child's name and address overseas and the dates of birthdays. If you have already applied to the BBC and have heard nothing for some months, you should write again, mentioning your previous application."

My mother advised us of the date and time. It was summer and when the day eventually arrived I was practising my high jump with Dennis for the forthcoming sports day. Mary called me inside.

Restless feet drummed on the bare floor as I listened to messages of love flying across the airwaves. The importance of the broadcast was completely lost on me and I wondered if it really merited my presence.

Eventually I heard my mother's voice, wishing she could see how big I'd grown and telling me she'd send me a picture of my brother Norris, in his cowboy suit and asking me to be a good girl. – Where had I heard that before?! - That was it. Thirty seconds and the next mother was on air. Before anyone could say a word I'd jumped up and rushed back outside, the mosquito door clattering behind me.

Dennis followed thinking I must be upset, only to find me already practising again.

"Did you like hearing your mother?" he asked.

"Was all right."

"Are you sad?"

"Why should I be sad?"

I think Dennis was a bit taken aback.

"Well I thought," he shrugged his shoulders, "as you hadn't seen her for a long time."

"But I like it here. It's my proper home. Will you put the pole back for me?"

End of conversation. England had been banished from my mind.

One weekend pops invited the Schrochinskis to the farm. While the elders were talking about the state of the crops and the price of pelts, Mike, Joe and I went scavenging. We found some old feed troughs behind the barn. They were just two barrels cut in half.

We each carried one down to the lake and found they floated perfectly. Using branches as paddles we were having a whale of a time. Suddenly Mike shouted: "I'm sinking!" Joe and I laughed, but the smiles were soon wiped off our faces, so were we. By now we were nearly at the centre of the lake and none of us could swim. There was a mad scrambling and splashing as we headed for the shallows. Barrels still floating – just! They gave up the ghost about five feet from the edge, but at least the water was only about two feet deep, so we were able to wade safely back ashore. It was a scorching hot day so we stripped to our pants and hanging shirts and dungarees on some nearby branches we raced around the pasture, knowing the hot sun would save our bacon.

No one ever found out and you can bet your bottom dollar we certainly weren't going to tell anybody. This time the strap stayed put.

We were walking back across the pasture, having a real good blather, when we noticed an eagle perched on a branch. It seemed to be staring straight at us with his piercing yellow eyes. We stood mesmerised, not daring to move a muscle. It's fierce talons, bigger than a man's hand, gripping the roughened bark. Suddenly without any discernible movement, it glided effortlessly away. We just looked at each other. "Wow!" gasped Mike. It said it all.

Only a month later Pops repeated the exercise but with a few other children as well. Three came on horseback and three came in a buggy. The horses were all hitched to some trees and we were left to our own devices.

I introduced them to Snowflake, my little heifer, then George Horvath suggested we hitch up his horse to the stoneboat. He put a barrel on top for Saul, a four-year-old with a tangled mop of strawberry hair. He looked most odd. The clothes he wore were so unsuited to him. They seemed to be standing up on their own and the body inside only incidental. We all clambered onto the 'boat' and George climbed on the back of his horse and we were away. The horse picked up speed and we had to hang on for dear life. It was great fun until we came to a hill. Getting up was not a problem, but coming down was another story. That horse hit it at full gallop. Most of the kids panicked and leapt off, the barrel skittered off and rolled down the hill with one bawling youngster inside. Fortunately we all escaped without a scratch, but decided that maybe we ought to try something a bit more sedate. We returned to the farm and were playing around the haystacks when we heard someone screaming behind the barn. We all ran to investigate and found the four-year-old had stuck his head in between the spokes of the buggy. Not as bad as we thought. He only had to lift his head from the narrow part to get free, but he wasn't old enough to realise that. As we'd had two mishaps everyone decided maybe they should head home.

At that moment Mary came out and gave us all a drink of lemonade. We'd have been in trouble if she'd seen the young 'un.

AUTUMN 1942

You always knew when fall was upon us because apart from the darker nights, weaker sun and colder air, the sky would be littered with birds on the wing to warmer climes. Especially the Canada goose with those incredible formations, and the noise they made!

I was helping Pops mend some harness near the main barn, when I heard the noise of an engine. Pops dropped everything and started to run towards the house. I followed. It was Herman, his brother with whom he shared so much for thirty years. They clasped hands warmly. Herman was the complete opposite to his brother. He was a small, neat, friendly character who gave of himself generously, especially in conversation. He readily admitted he was 'an old blatherskite.'

He came in to say hello to Mary and Auntie Mum, then he offered to take Pops and me for a ride to see some neighbours. It was threshing time, so we went to a nearby farm where we knew the team would be and he could catch up with some of his friends from the twenties and thirties. They had twin boys, Glen and Ben about my age. Although they were identical to look at, their personalities were completely opposite.

We were all helping the gang and the horses unexpectedly shied, rearing upwards and tipping the whole wagon of sheaves on top of the twins.

Men rushed to quieten the horses, but before they could start pulling the sheaves away, a blonde head popped up like a Jack-in-the-box, he never uttered a word, so they knew it was Glen, only to be quickly followed by sheaves flying in all directions and shouting even before he emerged. "Wow, guys, what happened." Definitely Ben.

Nothing could persuade Glen to talk. One time the boys were playing around the barn when the old Billy goat ambled over and nibbled the buttons on his bib and overalls. That goat would eat anything. Glen's trousers flopped around his ankles, but he just stood there, bottom lip trembling, while his brother was in paroxysms of laughter on the ground.

Normally the goats, they kept about twenty, were in the pasture, but something had spooked them and they'd scattered far and wide. They managed to round up a few but the farmers preferred goat to mutton!

George Haigh said he always kept a goat with his cattle. "When that Billy saw any of the Nadle's cattle heading for his territory he'd chase them away. The problem was" said George, "the stampeding cattle made a real mess, smashing through undergrowth and across pastures." He grinned. "Then Mrs Nadle would head straight over to my farm and give me a piece of her mind." He laughed out loud. "I suppose you could say our goat got Mrs Nadle's goat!"

But all things come to an end and one severe thunderstorm it was struck by lightening and killed.

There was also a mangy black and white goat, which no one seemed to own, so Charlie Cockle, the auctioneer, put it in his pound. "If nobody claim bloody thing, in fourteen day, it being auctioned."

He passed on the message to all.

On the day of the auction, very early in the morning, somebody came and stole goat, rope and stake.

Charlie was livid. "They could have left me bloody stake," he yelled.

The horse was the farmers ally, for if they fell ill or were in injured, work would almost come to a standstill. Take tree felling for instance. The trunk would have to be hauled to the stoneboat, after it's branches had been lopped off. Pops could fell a tree within inches of a specified point. The trunks were then hauled to the back of the house and stacked ready for sawing into manageable lengths. It would be chopped into dumpy, stumpy, squat little logs for our dumpy, stumpy, squat little stove.

While Pops was piling up the trunks, I would make sojourns back into the wood to collect all the branches, which had been chopped off on site.

It was then my job to stack and separate into neat piles. Green one side, dead the other. Served the same purpose as coal and coke. You needed sticks as brittle as candy to start a blaze and the green logs kept a nice even warmth.

WINTER 1942/3

The still air coated with frost heralded the start of another winter. Soon we would see wild animals much nearer the house. Herds of wild deer would scour the area for food. They have eyes as large as a horse and they can see an intruder miles away, then suddenly up goes the warning signal on the rump, a rosette of white hairs that can be raised and away the herd leaps of speeds up to sixty miles an hour.

Evidently this warning signal can be seen by other deer up to four miles away, so it affords marvellous protection against the marauding coyote. Unfortunately, the hunter can also spot it and with a high powered rifle can easily pick off his quarry.

But I had no rifle, I just wanted to observe and would spend hours downwind seeing how long it would be before the herd were alerted to a stranger in their midst.

Bucks would fight for mastery over the herd, locking horns in combat. The eventual winner would keep the wayward herd in check by thrusting his head and emitting loud, very strange grunting noises. He would keep his harem until he became weaker and a younger, stronger male would dominate him and take over the does.

I was taught how to trap and trail wildlife. Dad showed me how to skin and clean rabbits, weasels and wolves, then stretching and drying the pelts ready for sale in town.

The collection of wild flowers Mary had amassed during the summer months would now be re-created in water-colours. They were a joy and I tried very hard to emulate her work. But for some reason I usually preferred black and white. The wild rose was easy. A confusion of pink among the arboreal undergrowth, but the Lady's Slipper I could never capture with it's golden upturned mouth, turned to greet the oncoming day.

The real challenge was not of the flora and fauna, but the unblemished snowflake as it exhibited itself on the frosted windows. Everyone individual, extravagances of perfection like an exquisite diamond.

Yuletide was soon upon us, so Mary said we'd make some paper chains. Coloured paper was cut into pieces 6" x 1" and looped together and pasted with a mixture of flour and water. The resulting decorations cascading from the ceiling. I don't think they'd ever bothered before. Pops asked if I had any in my bedroom then suggested the horses might like a few in the barn. I put three short lengths down the dividing posts of the stalls, but next morning they were in pieces on the floor. The cats had had a high old time, flicking them around until they were virtually destroyed. I salvaged a couple of short lengths and put them outside the chicken coops.

Early on Christmas Eve, Pops would pick up the kerosene lamp and as always, invite me to help in the barn.

"We've got to get everything ready for Kris Kringle."

We would move Belle into Captain's stall and new hay would be scattered in the empty stall, troughs filled with oats and the floor covered with fresh straw.

After the daily bible reading it would be off to bed to await that special day.

That year I received a baseball bat and hat, also a string of raisins and candy. Another happy Christmas.

THOUGHTS

Pops never showed emotion, to his wife or children. He didn't seem capable of sentimentality, never showing emotion, but it clearly manifested itself in his actions of making Christmas such a magical time for me. Obviously deep emotions bubbled underneath that harsh exterior.

SPRING 1943

I couldn't wait to try out my baseball bat. Mind you practising proved a tad difficult, but undeterred, I would throw the ball into the air, give it an almighty thwack, retrieve it and clout it back again. It never occurred to me that it would have been considerably more fun with a partner.

Harvey, the second son, came home on leave, before departing with his regiment to England. I was out practising, when I was aware of a figure watching me. It was Harvey, leaning against a tree a felt hat dangling from his fingers. His dark eyes danced with amusement. "Want me to pitch a few?"

"Yes please."

While we were playing he told me that when he was younger he'd hit a baseball right to the end of town. "Charlie Limm measured it and said it had travelled over four hundred feet. But half the town joined in the argument as to whether it had bounced or not."

"Had it?"

"Couldn't say. I was too busy heading for a home run."

"How far's four hundred feet?"

He strode across the pasture, counting out loud. When he got to the end he asked me to pitch a ball and see how far he could swipe it. He missed the first completely, but the second soared high and far into a small copse. We never did find that ball.

But Harvey said he'd get Auntie Mum to order one from Eaton's catalogue for me. In the meantime I made do with a pebble covered in string.

On the second day he said he was off to see his friend Bennie Svenson.

"We'll probably go fishing," he told Pops.

As we had no car, he saddled up Captain to ride over to Bennies.

They rounded up a couple of friends and headed for Horse Lake, four miles east of Leross. There was always a great competition as to who could land the heaviest fish. On this occasion while no one was looking, Bennie stuffed a heavy glass bottle down the throat of his largest fish. When they got ashore it was decided Harvey and Bennie both had fish about the same size, but whose was the heaviest. Joe Nemeth was asked to referee. He picked up Harvey's and examined it. "You've got a good one there Harve. Could be a winner."

He then picked up Bennie's. "Mmm," he mused, "it doesn't look any bigger but by God it's a bloody heavy one." As he was speaking he squeezed it under the gills and the bottle shot out of its mouth like a rocket, nearly knocking Bennie sideways, much to the amusement of his pals. This tale has gone down in history and is still told sixty years later.

School was going well and the Sotski's came up with a great game after the teacher had left for the day. They would hitch up the ponies to the buggy and lead them to first base. Then everyone going south would pile on whooping and hollering, then urging the ponies at full gallop they would career around second, followed by third base, then hurtling in reckless abandonment, accelerate around the home plate, veering off right, up a slight incline onto the road and home. We would all be round the field yelling encouragement. One day they had just gathered momentum and were scorching around second base, when a sound like a machine gun rent the air. Every single spoke of a rear wheel had shattered and the whole thing capsized. Kids, books and pails flew through the air as if they'd been shot from a giant catapult. There were a few bruises and skinned hides, not nothing to cause concern. The rig had come to a grinding halt fifty yards away, as the ponies couldn't haul it any further. It lay there at a rakish angle, looking very forlorn, but not as forlorn as the kids, who knew retribution would be swift when they returned home.

Miss Lillico was informed of the incident and told under no circumstances was she to leave the school until all the children had left. They thought that would put an end to the shenanigans, but the teacher went north and most of us travelled east or south, so she never saw the fun we had with chuck-wagon races!

Only a few days after the accident the Choats came to school soaking wet after an unexpected bath. They usually came to school in a buggy, but sometimes three would ride on the back of a great, heavy piebald horse. They had to navigate a big slough, not normally a problem but this day the horse had stumbled, dislodging the rider at the back, who in his desperation to stay on pulled his two siblings off with him into the water. As they were nearer school than home they decided to carry on. Good job it was hot. They sat in class in their pants while their clothes dried on the bushes outside.

Only a week after the Choats soaking, we were messing about on the edge of the ravine, which ran along the area at the back of the school. Suddenly we heard a voice yelling; "Come back here. All of you NOW!" It was wildly gesticulating Miss Lillico, who was obviously quite agitated. We all scrambled up the bank and ran back onto the field. She rounded up all the pupils and then explained why she appeared so flustered.

Only a few years earlier a little girl called Rhea McEwan had been playing on a makeshift raft on the ravine and had fallen off and tragically drowned.

That news dampened our spirits and we filed quietly back to our lessons. By the next recess we were as exuberant as ever – but not near the ravine.

Dennis and that 'jump"

Harvey on leave

Baseball bat

Going to school on Belle

Mrs Nadle's Cattle

In the lake

SUMMER 1943

Another visit from Dennis, but this time he brought his wife Betty and eighteen-month old son Raymond. Pops was pleased to have some help with the heavy work. I found a wonderful new game with my little cart. It became a makeshift pram. On a small hillock about five hundred yards from the house I would propel the cart downward with Raymond tightly clutching the sides and I would see if I could beat it to the bottom. The problem was it never reached the bottom. Invariably, on it's perilous decent it would hit a rock or gopher hole, tipping it's cargo onto the grass. I sometimes rode in the cart as well, then we were both unceremoniously deposited in a hysterical heap. Our peals of unbridled laughter could be heard a mile away. Dennis and Betty had been out riding and came to investigate. Betty was convinced something terrible had befallen her son, but all she found was Raymond and I rolling around almost delirious with laughter. She was aghast, but Dennis told her not to spoil our fun. "They're having a wonderful time." He told her. "They'll not come to any harm. He's not falling far enough. Anyway," he concluded, They've been doing it for five days now without anything terrible happening, so let's leave them."

I don't think Betty was totally convinced but agreed that as they only had a day left and we were having so much fun, she reluctantly agreed we could carry on.

It's an odd thought, but here animals surrounded me and I had never given any thoughts as to how they were conceived. I watched chicks being born, wet and bedraggled and in minutes become small golden balls of thistledown, but never queried how they got in the egg in the first place.

I was in awe watching my first calf being born. This small, wet, furry thing tried desperately to scramble to its feet.

"Isn't that something?" asked Pops. I nodded but obviously looked completely bewildered. "Don't worry," he told me, "It'll soon learn to stand properly. It'll be walking as good as you and me in minutes."

I moved a little closer. "Pops?"

"Yes."

"How did it get there in the first place?"

Pops didn't smile a lot, but his face lit up with a huge grin and he actually winked! He still didn't answer my question.

I had watched the act of procreation but didn't understand what was happening, so when Raymond arrived on the farm aged eighteen months, I assumed they started at that age.

The farm was certainly a lot quieter when they'd gone but it didn't make me yearn for company.

About a week later I was in the big pasture, herding the cows home for milking when I saw one of our cows stuck in slough. There was no way it could clamber up the sides. I ran to tell Pops. "Dearie, dearie me. We'd better go see."

After reviewing the situation he decided maybe a bit of yelling and a few well-directed shoves would help it up the bank. No chance, it braced its legs and there it stayed. "Let's ride over to Jimmy Reids and get a thick rope," said Pops. We harnessed Belle and in twenty minutes were turning up the track to Jimmy's. Mrs Phillips, his housekeeper came to greet us."

"Jimmy about?"

"Yes, he's in the barn, mending some harness. What's up. Trouble?"

"Nothing we can't deal with. I'll go see him."

Pops jumped down from the buggy and strode towards the barn. Suddenly he turned. "No going in for ice-cream now, we haven't got time." He disappeared around the corner of the building. "Stay there," smiled Mrs Phillips, her eyes twinkled mischievously as she walked quickly into the house, returning at exactly the same time as Pops and Mr Reid. They were carrying a thick, heavy rope, she was carrying some ice-cream in a blue china dish, "Said we haven't got time," said Pops brusquely. Mrs Phillips winked and handed me a dish, whispering, "Come on, quick, eat it up, you'll be finished by the time they've got that rope in the back."

I did, just. As I handed back the bowl, Pops and Jimmy were climbing on the buckboard and his old dog leapt in the back. Slapping the reins hard on Belle's quarters we set off at a steady canter not stopping until we reached the pasture where the cow was stuck.

Pops and Jimmy tied one end firmly to the cow and the other to Belle. They yelled and slapped it on the rear while I urged the horse forward. Nothing, the animal refused to budge. Then I heard Jimmy call out, "Whiskers, here boy." His black and tan dog leapt from the buggy and ran to Mr Reid, "Go on boy, get 'im." He pointed at the cow. The dog raced down the bank and started yapping furiously at the cow's heels. In seconds the animal was scrambling up the bank and in less than a minute it was galloping towards the herd none the worse for its adventure.

Would you believe, after that ridiculous scenario, Pops could still only exclaim, "Well I declare," but Mr Reid did get a pat on the back.

Although many of the farmers had dogs, they were not of the working variety. Well not as we know it. Actually when I think of it, some of the dogs the farmers kept were quite a bizarre choice. For the middle of the prairies anyway.

The Haigs for instance owned a Pomeranian. It gets better. He only had one eye! It happened when he was chasing the farm cats, as one scuttled under an implement, which was too low for 'Sailor' and he ran into a protruding spike. The injury was so severe it resulted in him losing the sight of an eye. Mary Haig told me: "That animal was always getting into trouble. Only last week he'd been ferreting around the farm as usual, when I heard a whimpering at the door. There was poor old Sailor with a porcupine quill embedded in the middle of his nose. It was so deep, I had to use pliers to pull it out."

That reminds me of the time George Haigh also had a near miss with one of those animals. "I was out hay making," he told me, "not noticing anything lurking, I bent down, when the bloody thing attacked. Quills shot everywhere, but as luck would have it, my parka hood had fallen over my head as I'd bent over and all the quills embedded in my hood. That was some lucky escape, because they only missed my eyes by a fraction."

Porcupine is actually very tasty. Coyotes are aware of the danger and try to tip them over on their backs before attacking. Pops shot one once, intending to feed it to the cats and Buster, but suddenly a coyote appeared from behind a bush and snatching it up in his jaws, raced off.

Horses are particularly prone to quills. They'll be quietly grazing away, completely oblivious to anything untoward and inadvertently their muzzles touch the quills, which when released, move at the speed of an arrow.

George Haigh told me he'd seen a horse with over two dozen embedded in its face. "They can be over two feet long." He told me "and if they are not taken out quickly, they go in even deeper and are very difficult to take out and infection easily sets in."

But back to Sailor, that irascible Pomeranian. George said he was once arguing with a neighbour about the price of horses, "and Sailor was watching us intently and when it got heated (as most of George Haigh's deals were prone to do) I noticed the dog slinking away to a corner of the barn. When the farmer eventually left, to my satisfaction, I might add, I could see Sailor peeping out from behind some hay. I went over to him, when suddenly he stood up on two legs and wiped an eye with his paw." George laughed out loud at the memory, "He was only wiping his good eye!"

Still with the Haigs. Old man Haig (Bob) was nearly ninety when he was driving himself home in the buggy. Mary Haig took up the story. "The team shied when a stoat ran across their path. Both horses reared up in terror and lifted the buggy in the air. Dad was flung out and watched helplessly as the team galloped away, dragging the buggy on its side. He was bruised and sore but otherwise okay, so set off to walk home. When he arrived at the farmhouse, we told him off. 'It was only two miles home!' he said."

"Well he was only ninety!" chuckled George.

"We were a bit concerned though when he started complaining about a rather severe pain as he walked. Now there was no such thing as a doctor's visit in the prairies, mainly because no one had a phone. You had to ride into town or fix it yourself."

"Too right," said George, who continued with the story. "The buggy was long gone and it would ages before we could retrieve it, that's if was in a state to retrieve. I told Mary we needed to get Dad to a doctor pretty quick and suggested riding to a neighbour, about three miles away, who had a car. One of our horses was grazing near the barn, so Mary picked up a bridle on the run and in seconds it was on his head and she'd leapt on his back. I watched her gallop off, returning with our neighbour and his open topped Studibaker. We loaded Dad into the back without much of a problem and within an hour we were in town."

"Was he badly hurt?"

"Well, when the doc. examined him he said it was a miracle he'd survived the walk let alone the ride to the surgery. He'd only broken a vertebrae and he said if they'd driven over a bump of any size, it would most certainly have killed him."

George Haigh was so impressed by the car that he made some enquiries to see if it was for sale. "It was," he grinned "and the deal was done on a handshake. Oh plus a colt and two goats."

Knowing how much he loved his horses, I asked: "Was it worth it?"

"It wasn't a bad deal, but after a couple of years it started to be temperamental. Well Charlie Cockle the auctioneer had been telling me he had the best mare he'd ever handled, so I went to have a look. She was one of the best bits of horseflesh I'd ever seen. So I swapped the car. Boy was that some deal. I got two of my best colts ever from that mare."

"And the Studi?"

"Oh Charlie traded that for a plough and that was bought for cash. So everyone was happy."

Old Bob Haig made a remarkable recovery from the accident and for many years was a real asset around the farm.

Early one morning he'd gone out to help feed the pigs and chickens.

"My legs don't seem to want to work this morning George."

His son took his arm and helped him to a nearby pile of hay.

"Now, are you sure you're all right while I feed the hogs."

His father nodded. "I'm fine son. You carry on."

George completed the feeding, while still keeping a wary eye on his dad.

"Come on," said George, "Let's get you back to the house."

As they reached the porch, the seven-year-old great-grandson ran out looking concerned. "Can I help you Granddad?"

The old man paused briefly, smiling down at the tousled haired youngster. Cupping his small chin in his weather-beaten hands he gently spoke. "I can see you Dearie, I can see you." A wan smile crossed his face as he slowly crumpled in his son's arms.

Mr Haigh Snr. had died as he said all old timers should go. With their boots on. He was ninety-six.

As fall approached, the grass in the sloughs had to be cut with a scythe. They were really awkward to carry, Pops used to sling it over his shoulder but it often bashed into his backside.

When he'd cut all the grass, he'd have to bring the rake in, pulled by two horses, to lift them into bundles and I would help by forking it out. We were in the middle of a slough when the team trampled on a wasp's nest. They attacked everything in sight. The terrified horses were rearing and kicking, crashing the rake over on its side, throwing Pops heavily to the ground. The problem was, we were in a small gully with a steep incline and the horses couldn't clear themselves from the prolific undergrowth at the top. Pops and I scrambled up the bank fleeing the swarm, while the terrified team reared and crashed around. The harness became a tangled mess and the vegetation was literally pulled up by its roots. We watched helplessly as they careered at breakneck speed across a newly ploughed field. Once a horse got hold of the bit there was no holding them, especially when some very angry insects were pursuing them.

Pops and I were unhurt. I didn't even get a wasp sting. Pops did, one. Most had headed for the horses. We eventually found them over half-a-mile away, exhausted and dripping in sweat and still trembling in fear. It took a while to calm them down but a quick run down with some wheat straw helped. It took a little longer to clear the debris from the harness. We'd been very lucky. Injuries to the horses proved only superficial and they seemed none the worse for their ordeal. Only one trace on the harness was irreparable and the double-tree was smashed. Pops could make another, but time was running out.

With Raymond in cart

Betty and Dennis

Raymond

Photo of brother from England

One of Bob Haig's broncos

Sailor

AUTUMN 1943

Early in September before any snow had fallen, Uncle's George and Dick (Herman's sons) paid us a visit and asked if they could take me back to Wishart for a week.

Whenever they came to call, Auntie Mum made me wear a dress. Which did not impress me.

They had a splendid looking car, so I decided they must be very, very rich!

I wasn't too sure staying with them was a good idea. I'd have to wear dresses every day.

I climbed into the motor with my little case and we were off. We eventually arrived in the middle of a lumberyard.

"Come on, out you get, we're home."

Home?! But this was a lumberyard. Not unlike the one at the back of our little house in England, but a lot bigger. The thought casually flitted through my mind.

This home consisted of a large rambling apartment above the offices, reached by a wide, brightly painted staircase.

I had a wonderful action-packed five days, exploring the yard and visiting their many friends. On two evenings I was treated to the pictures. A real event in my life. I had no idea what to expect, but they made it sound exciting.

We settled in our seats, popcorn at the ready. The lights dimmed and the film opened with a face of Wallace Beery, not the most handsome face in the world. I physically jumped in fright at the sight of a twenty-foot face talking to me. After the initial shock of seeing giant people, I quite enjoyed the experience and eagerly looked forward to our next outing. This turned out to be Shirley Temple and I was entranced, the larger than life characters no longer menacing. You'd have thought I might have been tempted to show off my tap-dancing prowess to my relatives, as I had to the naval personnel on my way to Canada. But it never entered my head. Not important.

The next night we went to a concert called 'The Glee Club Hour.' It was organised by Aunt Alice and they performed a different show each month. She sang lots of comic songs and was in funny sketches. It was all great fun, although I didn't tell my Aunt Alice, the lady I liked best of all was called Lois who sang all her numbers stood on one leg.

Because of the success of these concerts the local radio station had asked my aunt to take part in their weekly show called 'The Gargle Juice Hour.' It was something in the Spike Jones tradition, comic situations and songs. Aunt Alice was used for her funny voices, but she came into her own with her impressive repertoire of whistling as backing for every song imaginable.

Although I had thoroughly enjoyed my week, I was delighted to be returning to the peace and quiet of the farm. But most of all I missed my animals and my practise jump. Mind you there was something I'd miss from Wishart. Those giant squashy settees they let me jump on.

It was fall and that communal thresher was on its way. Dawn had only just broken when they arrived. They wasted no time in getting started. The wagons groaned under the weight of sheaves, needing two strong horses to pull it. The thresher pounded away, tossing the valuable straw clear, while the grain was pumped down a wide tube into a waiting wagon.

Halfway through the morning, Mary and I carried large cans of coffee and some home-made pumpkin pie to the team. Have you ever tasted pumpkin pie? Definitely an acquired taste.

The men devoured everything we'd taken and were back to work in minutes.

I stayed to help, mostly leading the team to the thresher.

Mid-day meals were also taken in the fields, there was little respite. Slices of ham and beef – great chunks of home-made cheese and mounds of Auntie Mum's freshly baked bread. It was all washed down with gallons of thick, black coffee.

After lunch it was back to the thresher but the afternoon was fraught with mishaps. The harness on a team pulling a wagon full of sheaves snapped clean through. They'd just managed to find another harness when a wheel came off a wagon full of grain tipping the precious cargo onto the stubble field.

It didn't stop there. Just when they thought nothing else could go wrong, the belt came off the thresher. This delayed everyone, as the machine ground to a shuddering halt, the wagons piled high and sheaves kept rolling in. The machine was inactive for over forty minutes as they struggled to repair it.

Haloes of honeyed dust covered everything. As dusk fell the accumulation of sheaves was now more than the thresher could handle. No more could be done that day, so the men trooped wearily to the house.

They stripped to their waists and washed in the large bowls that had been put out, taking the water from the barrel, which had been warming in the sun.

They ate ravenously, talking animatedly about the various crops they had already harvested. When all had been devoured they individually thanked the family for the meal, then made their way to their sleeping quarters that I'd prepared with hay.

I slept soundly and was wakened by a hub-bub below. The first blush of dawn was peeping through my window as I hurriedly got dressed and ran downstairs. They were all seated at the table, tucking into breakfast. One of my over riding memories is the sight of plates piled high with corn-on-the-cob and a great chunk of butter sat on the top of the steaming ears, cascading down the sides in golden rivulets.

Once again morning meant my usual chores but in the afternoon I was allowed to help the crew.

Again the thresher was proving temperamental and the men were getting increasingly anxious. There were angry storm clouds hovering and they still had two more farms to visit. But finish they did. It was pitch black before they arrived for their evening meal. Wind stubble had burnt their eyes and chaff was clinging to everything – hair was caked in it, eyes smarted and stung – It got everywhere, pricking and irritating your skin for days afterwards. But they'd harvested every sheaf and were jubilant. They slept soundly that night.

Still tired from the rigours of the previous day, I lay cocooned in my bed watching the slumberous and golden sunbeams, drift around my room, when I heard the noise below. It was my friends preparing to depart. Hurriedly dressing I raced downstairs.

Breakfast had been completed and they were saying their brief farewells. Time was of the essence and with many acres to be harvested before the icy grip of winter engulfed us all.

I ran after them waving madly as they disappeared up the track to the next farm.

With George and Dick

Bringing in the snow to melt

The Grain store

George Haig on Binder

WINTER 1943/4

CHRISTMAS

I was able to buy Pops some of his favourite tobacco – a whole ounce – Every time I weeded the vegetable patch I was given a cent and Pops gave me a share of his spoils when he collected the bounty from the government for gophers tails (five cents each) and crow's legs (one cent a pair)

I also wrote a poem for all the family. As I'm typing them now I wonder what on earth they thought of my weird sense of humour. Oh and when you're reading them, remember I was only nine years old!

I WONDER WHY (to Mary)
Birds sit in trees,
I wonder what he sees,
I think I'll fly
High in the sky,
To see the grass and wonder why
The sky is blue and bees have knees
Why is grass so green?
What can it mean
High in a cloudless sky,
I see Miss Mary eating pumpkin pie.

BUSTER, BUSTER (to Pops)
Buster, Buster, where have you been?
To Leross and back to see the queen,
Buster, Buster, did you see
Anyone there to invite you to tea?
The cats have all missed you
They were terribly keen
If under the throne a mouse you had seen.
Buster, Buster did you know,
You'd have had to bend so very low,
When bowing your head to say your goodbyes
Before you were made into fat doggie pies.

COLOURS (to Auntie Mum)
Roses, sunflowers, violets and such
Are all very pretty and smell very nice
But I wonder if you would like them as much
If they smelt like wet and bedraggled mice,
If their colours were brown, grey, purple and fawn,
And petals were iron, all spiky and sharp,
But I bet you prefer a rose tinted dawn
Or the sound of a nice, sweet sounding harp.
But beware of pretties and anything nice
It might conceal some high, jumping lice.

That year Pops had made me another pair of skis as the others were really quite short. After Christmas dinner, which consisted of turkey, just like in England, I couldn't wait for permission to leave the table so I could try out my present.

The poles were made from aspen, which is a white barked tree, with long stemmed leaves that dance and rustle in the slightest breeze. Its bark provides winter food for rabbits and mice and deer browse on its leaves. Bears, once a familiar inhabitant of the prairies, also fed on its foliage. A multitude of birds nest in its branches and the Plains Indians used the straight poles for their tee-pees.

Pops had built his original log cabin in 1906 entirely of Aspen and now a friendly belt of them protected our house and here I was pushing myself headlong downhill, proving that this tree was an integral part of the prairies.

A very important source of income for all farmers was the pelts from all the animals living on the land, particularly in the winter, as most animals turned white as camouflage against predators, therefore dramatically increasing the value of their pelts. The large Jack rabbit and weasels were the most valuable of the smaller animals but the real prize was the longhaired wolf or coyote.

The farmer has always regarded the coyote, the most cunning of the dog family, as public enemy number one.

It all goes back to the early days when the settlers couldn't risk losing a single chicken to a hungry coyote. It looks like a scraggy collie dog with large upright ears, a long nose and very sharp teeth!

The bushy tail is carried at half-mast, never curled back like a wolf.

It can outrun any dog and apart from its incredible cunning, it does have a few other points in its battle for survival.

It is particularly prolific, raising six or seven pups at a time, both parents taking turns to look after them. They eat just about anything that moves and a fair bit that doesn't! It is the supreme scavenger.

They usually hunt in pairs, with one blundering after a swift footed rabbit or deer, chasing it straight into the jaws of its compatriot, lying in wait.

They are the natural predators of racoons, who normally live ten years or so and only escape the clutches of the coyote by climbing a tree. A racoon doesn't hibernate but it does try to double its bodyweight before winter, even if it means pinching a face the ever present dangers.

Pops taught me how to read tracks and choose suitable runs for my loop of death. I soon became an expert and was given my own territory. With my new skis I could now go further afield, searching for new runs and setting my own traps and snares.
Pops would set the larger traps for the wolves, but I would go with him to bring back the carcasses on a small sledge. Pops used to travel about on snow-shoes.
You could see the Jack-Rabbit watching us from what he considered a safe distance. I couldn't count the times I saw a pair of erect ears, pinkly translucent in the pale winter sun. Hunting rabbits is easy. He hides everything beautifully – except his ears.

THOUGHTS

A snare should be set four fingers (in my case five) from the ground and if correctly sat the animal was dead within seconds but there were instances when I was faced with the eyes of a terrified animal in great pain, but I never even flinched and would calculatingly twist it's neck and put it out of it's misery. Now I feel quite repulsed, but it was how we existed. It was survival, and I have to admit - rabbit stew was one of my favourites.

Going to town in the buggy

In the cutter

SPRING 1944

As I got older I wandered much further afield and this gave me a chance encounter with someone who has kept a place in my heart all these years.

I first noticed a thin coil of grey smoke spiralling above the trees and went to investigate. After pushing my way through fairly heavy undergrowth, I came across a path of sorts. It led to a small clearing with a neat log cabin on the far side. I stood on the brink. The smoke from a twisted, metal chimney, jutting out at an angle from the sod covered roof, drifted upwards like tiny, grey birds casting their down as it disintegrated gently into the endless sky.

Time hung suspended. There was a feeling of complete peace and serenity. Suddenly a man appeared in the doorway, wearing buckskins. He was tall and muscular, with long, dark blonde hair and a heavy beard straggling over a checked, blue shirt.

I stepped back into the shadows.

"No, don't go." His voice was kind and gentle.

I paused, not sure what I should do.

He smiled. "Would you like a mug of coffee?"

I shook my head.

"There's one on the stove."

I shook my head again.

"How did you find me?" He was motionless in the doorway.

"I saw your smoke." I replied in the softest of whispers.

"I knew it was only a matter of time." He smiled again. "Are you sure you don't want some coffee?"

"Yes thank you."

"Yes thank you, you don't, or yes thank you, you do?"

I wasn't quite sure about this situation. "I think I'd better go."

"Aren't you going to tell me your name first?"

I thought that was okay, so replied. "Dorothea."

"That's unusual."

I nodded again. "I'm going now."

"That's all right. But will you come back and see me?"

Shrugging my shoulders, I stepped back into the undergrowth, then turning quickly ran back to the farm and familiar territory.

My mind was buzzing with conflicting emotions. Should I return? Should I tell the family? I decided that was not an option, but my first question I found not so easy to answer.

The encounter was constantly on my mind but it was nine or ten days before curiosity got the better of me and I decided to pay another visit to my stranger in the woods.

I stood for several minutes on the edge of the clearing, watching the cabin, but no one seemed to be at home. I certainly daren't venture any nearer. Disappointed I returned to the farm.

Over the next few days, 'Beard', for that's what I decided to call him, was constantly on my mind. I was determined to return as soon as possible.

Curiosity was now the over-riding emotion.

Finishing the chores in double quick time, I decided it was now or never.

This time as I approached, I could see Beard sitting outside whittling on a piece of wood. He looked up as I approached. Both being shy creatures, our first meeting had been brief and faltering, but we now had a common bond.

"I wondered if you'd come back."

Standing only a few feet from him I shrugged my shoulders. He had the most remarkable blue eyes.

"Do you want to see what I'm doing?"

Nodding, I moved nearer.

He handed me a tiny, part sculpted weasel.

"Would you like it when it's finished?"

I nodded again.

"You don't speak much do you?"

I shook my head.

Beard burst out laughing. "Come on, let's see if a mug of coffee will loosen your tongue. You stay here and I'll bring it outside."

I could hear him moving around the cabin. I was still not sure I should be there, but he had such a disarming smile. He re-appeared outside, with two tin mugs filled with the strongest, blackest coffee I'd ever set eyes on. It tasted even worse than it looked or smelt.

I sipped, slowly, very slowly, a little at a time, until the mug was half-empty, then made my excuses to leave. I was enjoying being there but I wasn't sure how Pops and Auntie Mum would react to my new-found friend.

Only two days had elapsed before I found another opportunity to shoot off to my secret rendezvous. He was again seated outside and immediately stood when he saw me. Grinning broadly he asked, "You come for another mug of my coffee?"

I hesitated.

"That bad was it?"

I shook my head. "I'm not thirsty."

"Well if you don't mind, I'm having one. Do you want to come inside?"

I shook my head again.

"It'll drop off if you keep shaking it like that." Laughing he went inside. I slowly followed. Hesitating, I stood in the doorway watching him. His back was to me as he poured from the coffee-pot perched on the lid of a familiar pot-bellied-stove. As I watched the thick, black, foul smelling liquid cascade into his mug, he enquired, without turning, "Sure you don't want one?"

"No thank you."

My eyes wandered around the room. Everything had been hand-made. Shelves lined the far wall with provisions, mostly tins.

The bed consisted of planks raised about eighteen inches from the ground and covered in wolf skins.

Animal skins were littered everywhere. They were even casually nailed to the walls, creating perfect insulation. Keeping the warm out in summer and the cold out in winter and they looked great.

He turned but said nothing as he watched my astounded eyes voyage around the room.

"Well, what do you think to it?"

"Very nice."

He ambled over to a heavily carved rocking chair. The wood gleamed with a rich amber sheen. He draped a leg languidly over the arm.

"Aren't you coming in?"

Beard waved an expressive arm, rippling the fringes on his sleeve. "See that old chest over there?"

I nodded.

"Well you just go and have a look inside."

I moved a skin, casually strewn over the top. Fox I think. I lifted the heavily, richly carved lid.

It was full of woodcarvings. Birds, snakes, flowers, animals and trees. He'd sculpted them all.

"Go on have a good look. Take them out if you want."

I lifted out a tiny bird.

"Do you know what that is?"

"A Chick-a-Dee, I think."

"Good girl." He showed obvious pleasure. "But did you know they pinch the woodpecker's hole for its nest?"

I shook my head.

"Well they do and they line their nests with rabbit hair to keep them warm in the winter."

He unfurled his frame from the chair and sauntered over. He

pulled another carving from the chest. "Go on then, what's this," he asked, grinning broadly.

"That's easy. That's an owl."

"Ah," he wagged a finger, "But what sort of owl?"

"Just an owl."

"There's no such thing as just an owl." He admonished. "Do you know we have four types, and this little beauty is the most unusual of all. It's called a Burrowing Owl."

I scrutinised the carving more closely. "I've never heard of that one."

"Well this little fellah has no interest in trees at all. Give it the broad expanse of the prairie and you have a happy bird. It usually builds its nest in an old Gopher hole and lays up to ten eggs in a hatch."

"Does it eat mice like the rest?"

"Oh, boy I'll say it does. Main source of food for him, but they also eat insects. If you listen very carefully on a fine spring evening, you'll hear its whistle like calls wafting through the twilight."

I was hanging on his every word.

"What about the Horned Owl. Heard of him?"

I shook my head – again.

"Well he starts looking for a girl-friend as early as January."

"Why?"

He smiled and ruffled my hair. "You'll find out one day."

"I collect eggs," I informed him proudly.

"Do you indeed, well this owl is the only bird I know whose eggs hatch in exactly the order they are laid."

Beard knew even more than Mary. Mary! Oh heck. What if they're were missing me.

Hurrying to the door, I muttered, "I think I'd better go."

I ran swiftly from the cabin, not slowing down until I was nearly home, pausing briefly to catch my breath. I wanted desperately to tell them about Beard, but was still not sure how they would react. I decided I'd wait a bit longer.

I paid a further two visits to my friend. I learned about coots and mudhens, weasels and wolverines, a type of weasel, which could run as fast as a deer and fought like a cougar. It's energy was boundless and appetite enormous. Beard told me that when it spotted dinner it was virtually unstoppable and they were one of the few animals of which the wolf was scared.

It wasn't just the natural history I found so absorbing, but I found I was being given history and geography lessons without even realising.

He explained that many words were derived from the Indian tongue. For instance Saskatchewan was a derivation of Kisiskatchewan, meaning fast flowing river, "and what about bon jour?" he asked.

"Bon jour?" I hadn't a clue what he meant.

"Well the Indians have no equivalent of our good morning."

"Why?"

"They just think it a pointless thing to say."

"Why?"

"Because it's obvious you wish people that, so when the French Jesuits arrived to civilise the Indians they taught them to say, Bon Jour and this was soon absorbed into the language. The story goes that many years later the chiefs were summoned to meet high French Canadian officials in Ottawa, as the Indians walked into the big room, the officials greeted them with 'Bon jour.' That's wonderful,' said the Indians amongst themselves, 'they speak our language.'

He suddenly asked: "What's your surname?"

"Hudson."

"Hudson! Boy that's a really famous name."

"It is? Why?"

"The Hudson Bay Company established the very first trading post in furs nearly two hundred years ago."

"For the Indians?"

"Oh, no the white man came here fifty years before that."

"Did they only eat animals then?"

"Well it was an important part of their diet, but most of the first traders and explorers learned how to make a sort of chewy tobacco. It was originally made from buffalo meat – Boy that was some useful animal."

I told him a few years ago, when there had been a drought, the lake on our farm had almost dried up and Pops discovered hundreds of buffalo skeletons and wondered if they'd all been killed or succumbed to some disease.

"Most probably they had all been killed by the white man. At one time the government issued instructions for them to kill as many buffalo as possible. They were just slaughtered and left."

"What else were they used for?"

"Oh, boy, were do I start? Their hides were used for coats, tents and blankets. Their hair was woven into ropes and sinew made thread" He grinned, "Guess what the children used to do?"

"Chase them?"

He laughed even louder. "Not a chance, but when the herd had moved on, they were sent to collect their droppings, which they called 'chips'"

My face must have been a picture. "No, little lady, these chips were used to stoke a fire. They made excellent fuel. The buffalo meat was an important part of their diet, but the first traders and explorers learned how to make a sort of chewy tobacco, which could sustain a hunter for a day. They called it 'pemmican'. I make it for myself. Would you like to try some?"

I was very doubtful.

"It's nothing to do with tobacco. You just chew it like tobacco. It's made from the Saskatoon Berry, which grows along the side of the sloughs, you know the one with the blue berries.

I nodded. I knew it well. Many of the birds and some animals ate it in the fall.

"We don't eat it raw like the birds. First it has to be dried in the sun, till they harden. Then they're mixed with some meat, which has also been dried and pounded into a fine powder. Then all you do is pour a little melted butter over the mixture and hey presto! A ready made meal."

I was confused. "Why do you need it if you can hunt for food?"

"Because if you fall ill and can't get out, or maybe you're out hunting and hurt yourself, this could keep you alive for days."

He handed me a small grey slab.

I shook my head.

"No? Never mind, it doesn't taste of much anyway, but sometimes I boil it with some vegetables and then it has quite a nice taste." He continued. "And something else that's interesting. You know the little choke cherry trees around the edge of Sloughs?" I nodded. "Well if you boil the berries, you can use the liquid to write with. A sort of ink." I was spellbound, then again I realised I was spending too much time with Beard and I was now certain I didn't want anyone to find out.

"I've got to go and get the cows in."

He understood.

Two days later I was back. He greeted me enthusiastically. "Hi, Little Lady, I've seen a Beaver's lodge nearby. Shall we go se?"

I held his hand as we pushed our way through an overgrown path.

We waded through a meadow luxuriant in flowers. I could pick them without bending down. Butterflies rose and floated in a rainbow mist around our heads. I knew we were near water as croaking bullfrogs rumbled their distinctive greeting. I soon saw a male beaver chewing through the base of a small sapling. He is nature's master engineer. The lodge is half under water with many hidden entrances. The female carries her young for one hundred and ten days and they can swim immediately they are born.

The beaver has completely changed the shape of Canada's waterways. He is a workaholic, continually mending the dam and making renovations.

We watched him pick five branches in his mouth and swim out to the lodge paddling furiously.

As we watched this industrious animal, we were aware we were not on our own. Silently sitting by the water's edge, was the distinctively marked racoon. Known as the 'loner' or the 'looter.'

He eats anything, animal or vegetable, dead or alive. He is particularly dextrous on his toes. He often hunts for food without even looking. He feels below the waterline for snails or frogs, this knack of dabbling in the water comes completely natural to the cubs.

The male racoon started to tentatively walk across a broad log, which had fallen across the water.

The beaver pushed the branches to the side of the dam and silently stroked his way towards the marauding 'coon.' Suddenly he slapped his strong, flat, shiny tail, hard on the surface of the water, shooting plumes up to five feet high into the air. The startled racoon scooted back onto dry land and scurried through the undergrowth and out of sight.

Any trespassers on this beaver's patch could expect the same attention.

We silently stole away and were soon back in our familiar clearing. I followed Beard inside his cabin. As he was pouring out a mug of coffee I asked if I could try some more pemmican.

He handed over the grey lump, which I immediately popped into my mouth. A quick, 'thanks' and I skipped out of the cabin and headed home, chewing animatedly all the way. He was right, it was like eating bark.

As I happily ran into the house, Auntie Mum asked me what I was chewing.

"Pemmican."

"Pemmican?"

"Yes, Beard gave it to me." Oh, oh. Now the cat was out of the bag.

"Beard? Beard! What are you talking about girl?"

I told her about my friend in the woods. Her back straightened. I saw the disapproval in her eyes. She drew a deep breath. "Upstairs NOW!"

I winced at the ferocity of her words.

Looking out of my window, I had time to reflect on my impetuosity.

When Pops came in he was told about the incident. I was banned from ever going near those woods again. My impassioned pleas of "But he's nice," only seemed to incense them more. "If he wants solitude, let him bloody well get on with it then."

I'd never heard Pops swear before. I couldn't understand their intolerance. I felt a strange dull ache in the pit of my stomach.

To the adults he was an invader. His very seclusion, for whatever reasons, alienated him from these so-called mature citizens. But I missed him – a lot. In a child's innocence I had met a gentle caring man showing affection and deep understanding.

I didn't dare return, although I was sorely tempted on many occasions. My thoughts turned constantly to his tantalising smile and eyes that held a thousand secrets. I could see him sitting outside his cabin, under the star filled heavens and if I tried really hard I could even taste his dreadful, pungent coffee. But I had to rely on memories. The fringes on his buckskins that rustled and whispered as he walked, the steepling of his slender fingers when he listened intently, the corners of his mouth which crinkled when he smiled – which he did a lot - or simply the warmth and familiarity I felt in his company. What a loss.

The following summer, I decided enough time had elapsed and so with great trepidation ventured forth. Mainly because I was terrified I would be found out and also what would I find. I had never disobeyed my family before, but I had to take the chance. I needn't have worried. The clearing was already overgrown, the cabin in disrepair. The strikingly beautiful wood rose with its velvety blossom almost apologetically straggling along the crumbling roof.

He would have liked that. I felt a suffocating sense of awareness as I stood and surveyed the study of desolation.

I returned home, making my way along the tangled path remembering with deep melancholy his words and deeds.

THOUGHTS

In the ensuing years I felt deep remorse at being the agent provocateur, as I'm certain he would not have left of his own free will. I retained a nostalgic longing for this uninhibited, unconventional libertarian. Life can be so harsh and cruel.

Beard was a creative dreamer and communicator with a capacity for understanding, so where and why had it all gone wrong? Was there some dark secret in his shadowed past or had he just wearied of the chicanery of men.

We will never know.

SUMMER 1944

Most farmers supplemented their income in various ways. Cream, eggs, honey, apples, turkeys, even bottled fruit and jams. We bred mink, our Swedish neighbours the Eriksons, bred red and silver foxes.

When they'd originally come over they couldn't speak a word of English, so they admitted it was with great trepidation they made the epic journey. They were of farming stock so that was a bonus, but the language barrier worried them. Their daughter Joyce, was a friend of mine at school, told me how excited her mom had been at the prospect of coming to Canada, as she was dying to see how they laughed in English. But disaster struck when nearly all their stock escaped. Apart from the obvious value of the pelts, the neighbouring farmers were more than a little anxious for their poultry stocks.

A 'posse' was formed from the local populace and they went fox hunting. Sixteen animals had escaped. They managed to locate and shoot fifteen. The market value of the luxurious furs had been severely impaired as now they had a gunshot wound, but at least the Eriksons would have some return for their initial outlay, so all was not lost, but they did still have one marauding fox on the loose. He was free for several days, when an eagle-eyed farmer spotted him heading towards his hencoop and was able to shoot him before any damage was done.

Just after that episode two of our mink escaped. But we found out the hard way. While enjoying supper, we were alerted by the incessant shrieking of the poultry.

We had always had a problem with stoats sneaking in and killing our hens, so we all hotfooted it to the coop. By the time we arrived it looked like a battlefield. Corpses, blood and feathers were everywhere, it was absolute mayhem. At first we thought it must be several weasels, but their killing methods were much cleaner.

All was revealed when the mink runs were checked.

It was decided to try and tempt them back with some raw meat – poisoned of course!

All the meat disappeared the same night, but we never found the bodies. Two less pelts for us to sell.

Pops stayed guard for two nights but there were no further intrusions. It was a great relief because with winter approaching we relied heavily on the poultry for meat as well as eggs and we certainly didn't have enough money to buy any more.

I never tired of visiting Leross. Both the hardware and grocery stores were a revelation and Charlie Limm always rewarded me a pink striped, candy stick.

Even in the 40's goods were not always paid for but traded for produce such as butter, eggs and vegetables, which then hopefully, could be sold on.

The auctions were always fun and they were held quite regularly, especially if there were some young, strong horses available. Most of the local farmers came to an agreement with George Haigh, who was a recognised expert. He could tame any bronco brought to him.

We were in Charlie Limms when Pops asked me: "Want to go to the auction today?"

I clapped my hands in delight.

We walked over and stood at the side of a shed owned by a Polish farmer, with several youths sitting on the roof.

Suddenly there was this loud cracking noise and the whole roof collapsed. Wood and young men tumbled into the gathering below. They fled into the bush before anyone could recognise them. The Pole ran after them shouting: "Come on you skunks, who gonna pay for all dat?" Jim Cambridge the auctioneer, carried on as if nothing had happened. But boy that was some angry Pole.

New dawn, new day. On my way to school I would watch the high spirited hares shadow-box their way across the fields in a mutual display of fitness or listen to the frogs squabbling over their territorial rights.

Talking of territorial rights, there was a wild turkey cock, a giant of a bird, who strutted around on a small hillock, his tail fanned wide for everyone to admire.

All the animals kept well clear, even the stags stayed at arms length – or should that be antlers length?

That turkey was afraid of nothing and if he was spoiling for a fight, he would ambush his prey and charge. Feathers bristling, legs pounding, head held high and beak ajar like a two-pronged fork on attack.

I never gave him the opportunity to feel threatened, but I certainly admired him – from a distance! Actually that also referred to the domestic birds as well. They looked like vultures to me, I was sure if I fainted they'd have ME for dinner.

This particular morning, I had just waved to Pops as he was attaching the traces to the harrow in a nearby field, surrounded by dragonflies snatching their breakfast out of the air. What savage insects they are to be sure. Heading towards the hillock I passed the time of day with my swaggering friend, whose 'gobbling' could be heard for miles. I was passing on Pop's opinion of him. 'If there's one thing tougher than a wild turkey, it's a dead one.' He seemed to be duly impressed, when I was suddenly aware of a scream followed by an unholy racket coming from the field Pops was working in. As I raced along the uneven ground, I could see the team galloping away as if their lives depended on it. Pops was lying beside the upturned harrow and was just regaining consciousness. He'd been adjusting a trace when Bess had lashed out, smashing into his shoulder. Blood was already starting to seep through his jacket and he was very groggy.

I helped him up and putting his good arm around my shoulder, he was able to use me as a crutch. "Dearie, dearie me, Dot. It's a good job you're a tall, strong girl."

Never a truer word. I was already five-feet-five. In fact I only grew another quarter of inch. We made our painful way home. That was probably the longest half-mile of my life, and it didn't help when I tripped in a gopher hole. We stumbled and rocked for a second or two but luckily managed to stay upright. Mary was in the vegetable garden when she saw us coming, she quickly took over as the 'crutch' while I rushed into the house to forewarn Auntie Mum.

Once inside, Pops sat in his high-backed chair. He was obviously in great pain, but nevertheless managed to give me orders to try and locate the team and return them to the corral. I found them grazing not too far from the unfortunate accident. The harness was in a real mess, but luckily neither of the horses appeared injured. I unravelled the harness as best I could, then led them home and safely corralled them near the barn.

Back at the house, looking pale and shaken, Pops was drinking a mug of steaming cocoa. His wound had been cleaned and bandaged and the dislocated shoulder returned to its rightful place. Mary said Pops had passed out briefly when they did the 'deed' but never made a sound. "What not even 'Dearie, dearie me?' I asked.

He spent the rest of the day recovering. I was instructed to go to school and tell Miss Lillico that I would have to help on the farm until Pops had recovered sufficiently to carry on. The following morning he insisted on coming with us to the barn.

Mary harnessed the team and I drove them to the field. I was about to get my first harrowing lesson. Pops sat on the side, watching and instructing. At the end of three days he considered he was fit enough to work again. I was delighted that I was now reasonably proficient in handling a team of working horses, in fact the only farm implement I found it difficult to master was the rake. A small metal seat was sited right at the front of the implement, while the newly mown grass could be scooped up in great sausages behind you. You were only inches away from the horses backsides and it was not unusual to receive a smarting flick from their ever twitching tails or worse, especially if you were downwind when they started to pee! When we'd finished with the rake, it was usually my job to hand fork the grass into mounds and leave to dry.

With Buster

Taking in the hay

Bringing in the cows

Milking Vinny

On the dreaded rake

Ready for the fields with Pops

AUTUMN 1944

Winter set in really early and ice was already starting to form on the small sloughs beside the trails. These are an integral part of the prairie scene. They store the water which is essential for the grain, while the Aspen around its perimeter acts as a windbreak and gives protection to birds and animals. We were still going to school. Everything sparkled like tinsel. At the end of school our gang were running along the icy road, as usual making a huge racket. George was well in front and shouted: "Hey, guys, this sloughs frozen over."

We could see that the arched branches of the bullrushes were well and truly imprisoned in the ice so we decided it was okay to have some fun. Whooping and hollerin' we ran down the small incline. As we skidded along the surface, alarm bells started to jangle. The ice was cracking under our feet. We all froze in horror, not daring to breathe. There was an eerie silence as we stood transfixed. The ominous cracking stopped. We exchanged fearful glances. Dare we try to make it to the edge. A slight nod from Mike and I inched forward. It seemed to be holding firm. One inch, two inches, three inches. I glanced at Mike again, he smiled reassuringly. Right foot, left foot. Only fifteen inches to go. I was going to make it. The four immobile figures watched as I confidently slid another six inches. Snap. My feet crashed through the ice, plunging them into refrigerated water. Panicking I scrambling to the bank, luckily it was only three or four inches deep, but I got a lot wetter with my antics than if I'd just tried to step ashore. My friends were horror struck. They were stuck in the middle. Now what? George shouted: "Get something to try and test the ice and see if any is sound."

I soon found a heavy branch and went around the edge, bashing away to see how strong it was. It wasn't. I smashed the lot. That was really helpful!

George took control. "Grab hold of each other's hand and form a line. We'll try to make the edge bit by bit." They headed for the part I'd gone through, as we knew that bit was shallow. They shuffled nearer and nearer. Mike screamed out. "It's going." Everyone made their own way to the safety of the bank. They were soaked up to their knees, but furthest from our thoughts was the discomfort and numbing cold now creeping up our legs. We had to go home and explain. It was a very subdued group, which parted at the cross-roads. We all knew we'd be punished. Straps were common in all households. Ours as I'd already discovered hung menacingly behind the kitchen door.

Only a week after this episode, all the arched branches at the side of the slough were well and truly anchored in the ice. We could now tread safely in our crystal kingdom.

The pond became excursions of delight. We were the chaser, the chased, the hunter, and the hunted. We ran, slipped, spun and fell, playing ourselves to exhaustion. Often playing ice hockey. Branches would be our 'sticks' and one thing that made a perfect puck. A frozen horse turd. We didn't need a goalkeeper as our aim left a lot to be desired. My team was the Toronto Maple Leafs. They were my heroes and I had a scrap book at home, filled with cuttings from a magazine Mary had bought me – Oh and quite a few of the Dionne Quintuplets. Another scrapbook was full of their pictures.

The darkening pale lemon sky warned us of the impending night as the gentle sun stretched out its fading farewell. Waving, shouting, whistling and yodelling we would run joyously home.

WINTER 1944/5

The weather had been really severe, with temperatures reaching thirty and forty below, making sure we spent most of our time indoors. The cold was so severe that Pops continually had icicles hanging from his nose. They were suspended by the hairs hanging from his nostrils. I started calling him Poppy Icicle.

Huge ice stalactites hung menacingly from the roofs of buildings, some several feet in length. One day Pops was lifting the bar on the cowshed door, when a monster icicle came crashing down, nearly skewering him on the spot.

The virgin snow was used for drinks as well as washing - clothes and people, but it had to be melted down first, so it was my job to fill a small tin tub every day and transport back to the house. Thinking back I can't ever remember getting washed in the winter months. I supposed we must have because Auntie Mum was such a stickler for cleanliness.

One day, one of the cats had ventured out from the barn and her ears had frozen. Pops and I found her near the chicken coop and he carried her back to the warmth of the barn. He snuggled her in some hay, rubbing her body to bring back some feeling. As she warmed up the pain became so intense, she leapt up and went absolutely berserk, racing around the barn pulling crazily at her ears, the horses started rearing and were getting extremely agitated, as were the other cats. She was obviously in great distress, so Pops did the only humane thing and put her out of her misery.

If the weather was not too inclement, neighbours would venture forth in their home-made sleighs – or cutters as we called them.

One enterprising farmer had built what amounted to a shed on runners and to keep himself warm he'd put a small pot-bellied stove in the middle. You could see him coming for miles. Black, curling smoke drifted in the white landscape, as it belched from the small, black pipe protruding from the roof.

It sounds the perfect way to travel around that uncompromising landscape doesn't it? If there was such a thing as a negotiable road it might have been. His enclosed 'sleigh' only had a twelve-inch square gap for visibility, so he was unable to spot snowdrifts early enough. Consequence? The unstable vehicle would tip over. Every winter heralded the same cry from the farmers. "He'll not bloody get through this one alive." But get through it he did, winter after winter, but he did have some very narrow escapes. Two broken arms, a broken collarbone and a badly bruised shoulder. Oh, and a burnt neck from when his stove had fallen on him. It set his clothes and his transport alight. Luckily he was only yards from a neighbour's house and they were able to roll him in the snow and extinguish the flames. The little hut was ruined. Did he take that as a warning? Did he hell. In three weeks he was already building another. You might know he was a bachelor.

We had the normal type of sleigh, not quite as romantic as the ones you take moonlight rides in, but snug and efficient none-the-less. It was made of tin, bent and shaped to the shape of a shell, it had a bench seat, wide enough for two adults and one child.

The unforgiving winter dragged on, but snow was the farmer's friend. They called it 'white gold' because it lingered and seeped through the ground.

The settlers seemed to move easily with time. Pops had a fierce independence about him that seemed as one with the environment. I can picture this creature with a heavy woollen hat, ear protectors flapping against his stubbly chin; he never did them up or shaved properly. Another protection against the weather as he stomped around the farm. Come to think of it I never did up my pixie hood straps either. Copying him I expect. It had a pointed crown, which would bob about in the icy blasts. Those old timers knew a thing or two. That pocket of air at the top of the hood retained the heat escaping from my body, as all the best skiers will tell you.

Frostbite was a constant threat, but as everyone was aware of the danger, we were only troubled a few times, usually fingers because we abandoned gloves while setting traps and snares.

Inside the cowsheds it was warm and voluptuous, smelling of milk, warm breath and dung. It worked wonders for the sinuses. The cats were pretty impressed as well as we milked inside and they knew a quick breakfast would be waiting. Aiming a few well-directed teats in their direction resulted in a mad scramble for the airborne liquid. Very entertaining.

Apart from drawing, painting and adding to my scrapbook, I would spend hours playing 'Spillikins.' This entailed spilling a pile of used matches onto a flat surface, then picking them up one by one without moving another match. The slightest movement and it was back to square one. If they tumbled out, scattering loosely across the surface, I felt cheated as they could easily be recovered without a tremor and I liked a challenge – still do to this day – so with steady hand and immeasurable patience I would tuck away those tormenting sticks, again and again and again.

SPRING 1945

Pops and I had gone into town and were talking to Clarence Johnson, a great bear of a man. Barrel chested and legs like trees, he was renowned for his hard drinking and the subsequent fights he managed to incite. Suddenly we heard a commotion coming from the blacksmith's shop. Running with several other farmers we found two dogs attacking a fawn, which was tied to a stake, by a rope, in front of the blacksmiths.

Even with his lumbering frame Clarence was first on the scene, shouting and yelling at the dogs. But before anyone could beat off the frenzied animals, the terrified fawn had torn the stake out of the ground and raced in absolute terror up the main street, dogs snapping at her heels.

The fawn had originally been abandoned, so it was being hand-reared and it had come to rely on humans completely. It trusted them implicitly and could not now be released into the wild.

Ten or twelve townsfolk gave chase. They managed to divert the dogs, then they spread out to try and locate the young deer.

She was eventually spotted by Mr Choat, who gave a piercing whistle to the other farmers to let them know he'd found it. But in what condition?

They could see her spread-eagled across some bushes and quietly tried to approach her from the rear. She made feeble attempts to break free but was so exhausted the struggle was almost non existent. She appeared to be bleeding quite profusely from gashes and bites on her neck and haunches.

Clarence Johnson, with hands the size of shovels, gently lifted the terrified animal and carried it in his arms like a baby. At six-feet-five and 240 pounds (over seventeen stone) it was not a problem, but it was the compassion and care that Clarence showed to the fawn that surprised everyone. He was noted for his aggressive behaviour when drunk, but the town looked at him in a different light after that adventure.

The fawns wounds were tended, in fact some needed stitching, but she recovered completely was soon trusting her friends again. This time in a secure area.

About this time, our old dog Buster started being sick. Then he went missing. I spent hours trailing around the farm, looking in every bush and gully I came to. After a few days Pops said he must have eaten some poison. Mary told me that it's a well-known fact that dying animals will crawl away to expire in peace. One night during bible-reading we all thought we heard something outside.

"It's Buster, it's Buster," I yelled and ran outside. Nothing, so I started to walk through the small wooded copse near the house. That old barn owl nested there and I've told you she wasn't very happy if anyone invaded her territory and screaming from the safety of the night, she started to dive bomb me, but I was ready and shot back into the house. The next day I was up early to look for Buster again, but Pops had beaten me to it and said it looked like a racoon had been scratching around outside. Never did find him.

I asked if we could have another but Auntie Mum wouldn't hear of it.

Buster must have had a bit of Labrador in him, he was butter yellow like the corn.

I never lost my wonder at a field of corn, watching acre after acre turning into a palette of gold. They shone as if they were electrified. Sunlight marched through the brittle stalks as the waist high, ripening kernels nodded in the summer breeze, holding private conversations.

SUMMER 1945

The war in Europe had finished and hopefully everybody's lives there would return to normal. Well as normal as you could get after such calamitous events. Families had been torn asunder in the death and destruction, which had waged for five long years. Slowly the uniforms were being exchanged for 'civvies' and they had to return home to pick up were they'd left off.

Within the space of three weeks, Dennis and Harvey told Pops that they were not returning to the farm but would be seeking their fortunes in British Columbia and I was now expected to return to Yorkshire.

The family received a letter from England. Pops, Auntie Mum and Mary, sat me at the scrubbed, kitchen table.

"We have a letter from your mother which tell us the date you have to return to your family."

"But you're my family." They all exchanged glances. "Can't I stay?"

"No, I'm afraid you can't. You're to return in July."

I pleaded with them to write a letter to England asking if I could stay.

"Well we could ask, as we'd love you to stay and we will be moving to B.C soon."

Mary interrupted excitedly. "And you'll be able to learn to ice-skate properly,"

She was given a withering glance from her parents.

"Your real home is in Hull," explained Pops.

They didn't have to hug me to know they felt great affection for me. I knew they considered me almost one of their own and wanted me to become a true family member permanently.

They hurriedly penned a letter to my parents asking if there was any chance of me remaining in Canada, as they had already decided to sell the farm and head for Vancouver to be near Dennis and Harvey. Pops rode into town to make sure it got there as soon as possible.

We received a reply by return. It was sharp and to the point. 'Arrangements have already been made. Please make sure my daughter is on the transport reserved. I do not want her to remain with you in Canada,' and just signed, 'Dolly.'

I did not want to go. Everything I loved and understood was in the wheatlands of Saskatchewan. But my adoptive parents had no choice – I had to be returned – like a parcel – the way I'd arrived.

A brown tin trunk was packed with all my worldly goods. Clothes for the journey were separated into that battered, brown suitcase. The fateful day arrived and I was told I must wear a dress and a hat. It had been especially purchased for the trip. I hated it.

Everyone wore their Sunday best. Pops even wore a collar and tie and flat cap of course.

It was a baking hot day as we solemnly climbed into the buggy for the last time. Not a word was spoken. Driving along the dusty track, we were treated to a celebrity of song from my feathered friends. It seemed a special farewell, something of a bonus for me to remember when I walked the dark, city streets.

Through the haze of the summer heat, we could just distinguish the towering, red grain elevators, in a seemingly endless plain of sunlit gold. Leross loomed nearer and nearer. I felt tears welling in my eyes.

The horse and buggy were hitched to a post and we despondently walked the few yards to the station platform. I turned and Belle, our shaggy grey mare, seemed to be watching me. I ran back and threw my arms around my friend's neck. Was there nothing I could do to stop this happening?

It seemed almost poetical that we were cast in heavy black shadows from the prairie's most distinctive landmark. The wooden platform echoed to our heavy steps as Mary lined us up for the final farewell photograph. We posed with a semblance of enthusiasm as our melancholy state was recorded for posterity.

A barely audible sound split the stillness. Just discernible on the horizon were the unmistakable lines of an oncoming train.

Mary started to cry. Still no one spoke or moved.

A shrill whistle heralded its arrival as it shuddered to a halt.

I was the only waiting passenger.

Pops strode purposefully forward and handed my trunk to a smiling, black porter. Mary clasped me tightly for a few moments then, as she straightened up I could see the pain in those luminous, brown eyes. She suddenly reached forward and slipped a small packet into my coat pocket. "There you are" she said, "so you don't forget us" and turned briskly away. Auntie Mum just squeezed my shoulders and told me to be a 'good girl.' (Now where had I heard that before?!) Adding, "Don't forget, always trust in God." And as her lips brushed across my brow, she handed me a small bible.

"Come on, they're waiting," said Pops. His voice gruff and broken, lowered and shrank to a whisper, as if drawing him into a dark valley he didn't want to enter. I looked despairingly at them. Kissing me quickly on the top of my head, he almost pushed me onto the train. This was the only time in five years he had physically shown me emotion. It was all too much. I was overwhelmed and could only produce small-strangulated sounds.

With an extravagant whistle, the train pulled away, I stood motionless as everything I held dear dissolved before my eyes. I was numb with despair.

A guard led me gently inside. As I sat numbly on the seat, I remembered the packet. I opened it. It was a selection of photographs encapsulating my time with them, including a portrait of Mary which she'd had taken in Leross a few weeks previously. They compounded my grief even more. The journey to Halifax took two days. I hardly stopped crying.

I remember sitting at a window in the early evening watching the setting sun drift through flamingo pink clouds as they slowly vaporised into the far horizon. It descended lower and lower until it vanished forever. A black coverlet had been thrown over my world.

The guard, who had befriended me at Leross, did everything possible to ease my journey of discontent. He would bring me special tit-bits to tempt me to eat. Thin spongy sandwiches, especially made. I hated them. My heart cried out for some thick, fragrant, brown bread, lathered in butter and golden syrup. Was this cardboard really bread?

I returned home on the Ill de France, docking in Glasgow only five and a half days after setting sail from Canada. Research told me it was the quickest homeward crossing of all the troopships – it would be wouldn't it?!

The first evacuees returned home in April 1945. They were in mid-Atlantic when the news broke about the Nazis surrendering and two days later, five German U-boats surfaced alongside the convoy and surrendered to the Commodore. By May, 680 children had returned from Canada. The last evacuee landed in February 1946.

I was curious as to how many decided, for whatever reason, to stay in Canada. Again research disclosed that 1535 children sailed over to find refuge in Canada and it was reported that 209 evacuees decided to remain.

The return was unmomentous. I was sick most of the time and lay distraught in my cabin while kindly ladies fluttered around trying their best to revive my flagging spirits.

We were welcomed in the Clyde by Fleet Air Arm planes.

Upon arrival at Glasgow, I was ushered into a train, which

whisked me to York and my waiting relatives. My feet had hardly touched the cold concrete of York station, when strange people enveloped me in great bear hugs. I was made a great a great fuss of – It was not reciprocated. My heart was three thousand miles away on Grange farm.

As there was an hour before the train to Hull, we went to the station buffet for some tea. Tea! I hadn't had tea for five years. I sat quietly among a chorus of clatter. Auntie Kath, my mother's sister, ordered cream cakes, as she'd seen me watch fascinated as a lady on a nearby table bit into a chocolate éclair, leaving great chunks of cream attached to her cheeks like redundant marshmallows. A flat, strident, inharmonious cacophony of hullabaloo and ballyhoo. I felt like an orphan who'd been allocated a new family. But this disorientated twelve-year olds heart did not want a new family.

When we arrived in Hull, it took about twenty minutes in a trolly bus to reach our typical, inner city, two up, two down terrace house. At least ours boasted a small-untended five-foot square, plot of earth at the front, surrounded by a wild-looking privet hedge.

I was shown my bedroom, with one small bed, which was to be shared with my younger brother – When I looked out of the window, the sky had gone. I was staring at bricks, bricks and more bricks.

I found everything dirty and incredibly noisy. It took months to come to terms with the stew of humanity and its incessant din. Radios, children, dogs, traffic, banging doors, shouting people, it seemed endless.

The leaden skies and the never ending cold and damp depressed me even more.

My thoughts turned repeatedly to the birdsong and the fields of swaying corn. The utter stillness. It now seemed like a dream.

I realised I'd been bobbing along gently on a tranquil river and now there were rapids ahead. I had no choice, I had to spill over and be tossed around in the whirlpool of life.

During my time on the prairies, I had never encountered envy or hate. I had never craved possessions or became dissatisfied with my lot. The space, beauty and solitude of the Canadian wheatlands affected my attitudes for the rest of my life.

No toys, no comics, no playmates, no running water, no electricity, no toilets, no holidays, no money.

Experts today would be unanimous in labelling me 'underprivileged.' Underprivileged. Me?

Oh, no. They've got it all wrong, because I consider myself to have been a very privileged child indeed.

But now I was to be citified and prettified.

With Auntie Mum   The last goodbye

Canadian National Flyer
Saturday 14.7.45 - 11.15 a.m.

Citified and prettified

Mary
The portrait taken one week before depatrture day

1946

Allan, Violet and Mary Collingwood did retire to British Columbia, joining Dennis and Harvey, who were now in real estate.

MY FIRST LOVE AFFAIR –
With Canada and nature

House and barn in a field of corn

Sensitive man has always found pleasure in the sights and sounds around him, whether it is the tumult of crashing waves or the elusive colours of a butterfly.

I couldn't wait for Pops to shout, "Right time to bring the cows in for milking."

Heading off towards the meadow, I would easily be side-tracked. Stretching out in the entanglement of nature, nibbling on a succulent stem of the meadow grass, surrounded by a wild profusion of colour coiled around the stalks. I would watch big, fat bumble-bees and graceful butterflies glide from flower to flower.

A panorama of insects flickered and ambled around my world. Swifts dipped and skimmed in the breeze, while the Meadowlark with its yellow tummy and neck was a frequent visitor. You knew spring had arrived when you heard its distinctive song drifting over the pastures.

Before the plough turned the fertile soil, the prairies must have been a riot of colour. The variety of flowers was astounding. One of my favourites was the 'Nodding Onion,' a cluster of about ten, pink, lily-shaped flowers on the end of a very slender stem, which as the name suggests, were perpetually nodding. They grew in great profusion near the main cow pasture along with the rich yellow fronds of Golden Rod. Then there was there was the Black-eyed Susan, prolific among the meadow grass. Its striking deep orange petals and deep mahogany brown centre, insisting on your attention. In the late 40's, the singer Guy Mitchell topped the hit parade with a catchy tune called, 'Pretty Little Black-eyed Susan,' It never entered my head at the time that it was about a girl!

One of my favourite birds was the Hummingbird, its wings a blur, while with perfect control and absolute precision, it would plunge its beak into a beckoning flower. Thirteen times a second it whips its tongue in and out, eating every ten to fifteen minutes, because it expends so much energy reaching the nectar. It eats nothing else and this tiny, exquisitely sculpted bird flies to Mexico and South America for the winter.

Bold, but very wary, Magpies screeched overhead, preparing their nests, which is very similar to the crows. Mainly sticks and twigs. The inside is plastered with a coating of mud and lined with fine rootlets. It is completely fortified against predators by being completely roofed over by wickerwork of sticks. They can lay as many as nine eggs at a time. A sort of grey colour with brown splotches, looking for all the world like dried mud.

I was an inveterate collector. Birds eggs, nests, odd stones, feathers, flowers, leaves and unusual grasses. They were arranged in a selection of wooden boxes, made by Pops. The eggs often nestled in an original nest, but never scavenged until the young had flown. I managed to collect most of the birds, indigenous to our area, but never one from the king of the skies – the eagle.

Eagles, possibly the most versatile predator in Canada, could often be seen swooping down from cloudless skies. Their prey could be mice, rabbits or birds, particularly the chicks that were abundant on the lake.

Ridiculously easy prey was the Wood Duck. It lives in a tree hollow and the babies fling themselves out of the tree, directly onto the water below and start to feed immediately, as their mum is unable to perform this task.

You can imagine, the sound of plopping chicks falling from the safety of the nest, attract predators and of course mum was already on the water. As they instinctively plucked and picked at the water plants, they were a ready dinner for Mr Eagle.

The Coot, a small grey bird, was a particular favourite dinner of his. They would desperately try to gather as a flock, but there were always a few small ones and the ill-fated straggler could be seen diving and surfacing trying desperately to escape from the persistent eagle. When it became exhausted the victim would be unceremoniously snatched up, and soaring upwards, it left as quickly as it came, its prey struggling in terror in those brutal talons.

I took great pleasure in watching the wheat, oats and barley ripening in the hot summer months. Wheat took a hundred days, Oats and barley a little longer.

Hay was also harvested and I liked nothing more than to carry hay into the barn, you were embalming summer in your arms. It has a sweet, heady smell, still evocative to this day.

In the winter life was ordered and peaceful. In early May, all the birds I had watched the previous fall, almost blackening the sky as they winged their way to warmer climes, were now returning home. The call of the cuckoo and you knew it was spring.

The noisy shafted woodpecker, it's beak pounding against nearby trees, making holes where the hen could safely lay her glossy, white eggs. Often up to eight at a time. Woodpeckers are particularly fond of ants, which was very handy, as we had a great mountain of a 'hill' at the back of our house. I would cut part of the hill away and watch fascinated as they hurried and scurried with their eggs, often bigger than themselves, to safer quarters.

I've related a story in 'Beyond The Brave' where Pops brought some ants into their log cabin, hoping they would guzzle up the fleas they had. But it didn't work, so they ended up with the place over-run with ants and fleas.

On of my favourite birds was the Oriel. It's beautiful orange plumage could be easily seen flashing through the foliage as it burst into life – That's the buds not the bird!

The swooping Swifts and Swallows came in their hundreds. The Barn Swallow seemed to enjoy human company. Their diet consisted entirely of flying insects. I used to watch, mesmerised by their arial acrobatics, as they took lunch in flight. They usually had two broods a season with up to six eggs to a nest. I seemed to be endlessly watching chicks on their inaugural flight.

The humble crocus was considered the harbinger of spring to all prairie dwellers. It hardly waits for the snows to melt before bursting forth, converting a seemingly dead land into a carpet of pale lilac in a matter of days. They bloomed before the grass took over. A sure sign that summer was just around the corner. The prairie crocus isn't a real crocus at all, bearing no resemblance to the cultivated variety. I think the correct name is the Pasque Flower.

Another early riser was the ubiquitous dandelion. It grew everywhere. Near water it could rise to over six-feet in height, but if moisture was scarce it clung close to the ground. Livestock loved it. We used the young foliage in salads, while the flowers made a sassy, but very potent drink. And what pleasure I derived from blowing dandelion clocks. Without doubt one of the most useful plants on the prairie.

These were closely followed by the Indian Chief, a large cluster of reddish flowers, complimenting the tiny golden buttercup, often seen trying to raise it's head above the entanglement of wild strawberry plants, it's delicate yellow and white flowers disappearing to be replaced by small, but very sweet fruit. The ever-smiling violet eloquently stated the arrival of lighter nights and warmer days.

There were several lily type flowers on the prairies. The Western red, a magnificent flower dotted with black, growing to about two feet high. It was officially declared the Flower of Saskatchewan in 1941.

The official bird of the province is the Sharp tailed Grouse. It's speckled and splotched plumage is perfect camouflage. I've already told you about the time Pops and I watched them perform their ritual dance.

Their nests are built in grassy vegetation, laying ten to fifteen, olive coloured eggs in one hatch. It stayed with us throughout the year, surviving the winters well. To protect themselves from the severe cold and wind, they would plunge into a deep snowdrift and sleep it out. Pops often put some straw near their habitat, just as a little extra protection.

But probably the best known bird outside Canada, is the Canada goose.

What finer sight than to see a wedge of geese flying overhead at the onset of spring. Their wild calls floating through the sparkling air.

ART
WORK
FROM 1940 to 1945

My Indian! (A Blackfoot)

The Sacred "Ghost Shirt"

Deer and Fawn

The road to Bob Haig's

Mary sweeping out the house

Skunk and young

Squirrel

Coyote Pup

Fencing without nails

"50 YEARS ON"

In 1970 I returned to Canada and visited Uncle Herman, who was as sprightly as ever at the age of ninety.

He told me about the pain felt by his brother and his family on my departure.

He said, "I asked Allen if they were all sad." 'Never felt anything like it,' he told me. "Then went on to say that for the first time in five years he kissed you."

Herman grinned, "mind you he did say it was 'only on the top of your head! He told me he thought of you as one of his own. I had to console him." Another grin. "My big brother and I was consoling him. I asked him if they watched the train go? 'We just stood there,' he said, 'nobody moved until it was out of sight."

"You bloody didn't cry did you? I asked him."

"We all did." he said simply.

Herman showed me an account he had written of his life. It chronicled his time in East Yorkshire (1880 – 1904) and as a pioneer in Saskatchewan. He gave me a copy but he died before I could check some important facts, so in 1990 I returned to Saskatchewan and interviewed relatives of the old timers, who were such an important part of his early days on the prairies. They had also collated a huge book of stories about those days and I was able to add a great deal more fascinating anecdotes. All this has now been transformed into a book, Beyond the Brave'.

Allan Collingwood (Pops) died in January 29th 1961 at the age of 86.

Violet Collingwood (Auntie Mum) passed away on April 29th 1982 – Aged 92.

Their three children Dennis, Mary and Harvey were alive and well in 2001

Herman Collingwood died in 1980, only two weeks before his hundredth birthday, but his devoted wife Julia passed away in 2000, at the age of 105. Proof of the old adage: 'Hard work never killed anyone.'

Grange Farm House

The Beaver Dam is still there

Now home for a family of muscrats

On the road to Grange Farm and the prolific choke cherries

Inside the old house on the original bench holding a
'pelt stretcher' found on the floor

About the author

Dorothea now lives in East Yorkshire with her husband Ray and two Siamese cats. Her son Adam is an actor.

She has completed four other books – details overleaf.

Her next book 'Bands, Booze and Ballrooms'
is due out at Christmas 2001.
It's a nostalgic peep into the dance-band era,
full of anecdotes and photographs from 1940 to 1990.

Other books:

Buttocks, Boobs and Bedpans
A comic look at the medical profession and their patients in Hull and East Yorkshire. (with numerous cartoons)
Price £6.99

The Shocking Truth
Another humorous insight into the lives of Yorkshire folk, this time through the eyes of a market researcher. (with illustrations)
Price £6.99

Travel, The Celebrity Way
Anecdotes from 130 famous personalities, including, Rolf Harris, Matthew Kelly, John Nettles, Richard Branson and John Prescott MP. You're regaled with tales of hysterical honeymoons, cocky camels and paralytic porters, with a sprinkling of murderous mountains, broken bones and galloping goats.
Price £6.99

All the proceeds from this book are donated to charity, so Dorothea is indebted to all the personalities.
Price £6.99

Beyond the Brave
From Britain to bears, blizzards and buffalo.
A powerful portrayal of Canadian pioneers 1880-1946.
(Available from September 2001)
Price £7.99

The books can be obtained by writing to:
Buttercup Press, Ferry Road, South Cave,
East Yorkshire, HU15 2JG

Please add £1.20 for postage and packing (UK only).
Cheques to be made payable to T. James.